SHOW UP LIKE YOU MEAN IT

Show Up Like You Mean It

Paula R Jenkins

DEDICATION

This book is dedicated to Dectrick and Cheryl -

thank you for loving me as my authentic self.

Contents

Show Up Like You Mean It:

Living, Leading, and Speaking Your Truth

Paula R Jenkins

"Sometimes, people don't have hope, can't see hope, and are afraid to move forward. I do what I do because I want to help people see a different way."

—Paula R Jenkins

Foreword

By Bert Oliva

Paula R Jenkins is a force to be reckoned with, and I mean that in every positive way possible. She is beautiful inside and out, utterly brilliant, and a woman who is unwavering in her beliefs. If I had to choose one word to describe her, it would be "authentic." That is why when she asked me to write the foreword for her book about living and leading authentically, there was never a question. The answer was yes.

In *Show Up Like You Mean It*, Paula provides concrete tools and techniques to stay true to yourself, lead teams powerfully, and improve your emotional intelligence. However, this book is so much more than just a manual to develop your leadership and interpersonal skills. It is also the amazing story of a woman who has gone through numerous challenges and built a life of abundance by living in alignment with who she is at her core.

This book is so powerful because it is a testament to what Paula lives by—authenticity. By reading these pages, you will get to know her—the successes, the failures, the growth, and everything in between. As always, she is unapologetically herself while still teaching and exuding an unwavering love of others and dedication to improving how we connect and communicate with each other.

Besides being a well-written book with well-researched *and* well-lived insights, this book will also help you learn more about one more thing—yourself. The questions she asks you to contemplate and the activities she has you work through are deceptively simple at first glance. However, as you start to work through them, you will realize that you are not only internalizing the concepts from the book, but you are also getting to know yourself on a level that few of us ever do consciously.

Read this book. Connect with yourself. Connect with others. And as Paula says, don't "shrink to fit places you've outgrown."

Live Life, Don't Let Life Live You,

Bert Oliva
Global Speaker | Leadership Expert | Author |
Owner of BOWAstudios
May 2026

Acknowledgments

This book was written over years of conversations, growth, reflection, frustration, healing, leadership lessons, and truth-telling. I began writing this book in 2021.

To everyone who encouraged me to keep going when this book felt too big, too personal, or too unfinished… thank you.

Thank you to my very early reader, my husband, Dectrick Jenkins, for giving me the truth! It has come a long way. I appreciate your love, support, and push throughout this process.

To my daughter, Cheryl, thank you for being one of my greatest motivations and reminders of why authenticity matters. Watching you grow has challenged me to continue growing too.

To my dad, who often reminds me, "I'm still here!" — I am so glad you are. You are as authentic as they come.

To the people who trusted me with their stories, leadership struggles, hard conversations, and moments of vulnerability — you helped shape this book more than you know.

To my clients, audiences, coaching participants, colleagues, and community: thank you for allowing me to do work I deeply believe in. So many of the lessons in these pages were strengthened through real conversations and lived experiences with all of you.

To my advisors, readers, and supporters who gave feedback, encouragement, and honest perspective throughout this process — thank you for helping to sharpen both the message and the mission.

I must thank Desiree Mittman and Bianca Jackson for simply asking, "When is your book being published?" and forcing me to pick a date! I will be forever grateful to you both. Thank you!

Thank you to Dr. Tracy G. Crump, who over three years ago helped me get through the first version of this book. I am eternally grateful.

Thank you to my other early readers whose feedback I took in and used to adjust the manuscript: Cortnee Sanders, Karen Voelker, and Esther Mino. I appreciate you more than you will ever know.

Thank you to my village, who held me down so many times by co-working with me, texting me, and checking in to make sure I got this book done. Dr. Angela Shuttlesworth, you are a gem. Thank you for the daily check-ins — they mattered. Dr. Erika M. Brown, thank you for the push.

Thank you, Ama Griggs and Ayinde Martin, for helping me through this process and getting me to the finish line. Your encouragement, time, energy, and excitement for this project put a spark in me that wasn't there before. Thank you!

I also want to honor the memory of my dear friend, Nikel Cleaves, who encouraged me nearly four years ago to finish this book and put it into the world. She saw something in me that I was still learning to see in myself. I wish she were here to see that I finally did it.

And finally, thank you to every person reading this book.

I have asked this question many times over the years when I speak: "What do people get when they get you?" How you show up matters.

My hope is that these pages challenge you to stop shrinking, stop performing, and start showing up fully as yourself.

Because the world does not need more perfect leaders. It needs more honest ones.

— Paula R Jenkins

Introduction

What Is Authenticity and Why Does It Matter?

"I know a woman who goes to work every day dressed to the nines, attending every meeting, staying late for work, and wearing the mask that she is performing at her best, but she's tired and not being her authentic self. That same woman feels like she must perform at the highest level. Imposter syndrome is real." —Paula R Jenkins

"I wish I'd had the courage to live a life true to myself, not the life others expected of me." #1 Regret of the Dying, Bronnie Ware, *The Top Five Regrets of the Dying*

There I was, in a boardroom, confidently saying something I didn't even believe. As soon as the words left my mouth, I realized I'd become the poster child for inauthenticity. Honestly, I sounded so corporate, even my own mother wouldn't have recognized me! While I don't quite remember what it is I said, the topic, the date, or even the circumstances, I do remember that sudden realization—*this is not me*. I knew it was time to fire that version of Paula, and I did! I also realized that authenticity isn't about perfection; it's about permission—allowing yourself to be *real*.

But why do we even need to talk about authenticity?

It's because most of us are still editing ourselves to "fit." Many of us are not living our best lives because we can't or won't show up as our authentic selves. And why is that? Well, some might be afraid of the reaction; we've all witnessed someone showing up as their authentic self, only to be told something is wrong with them. Society often rejects authenticity and warns us not to go down that path. However, the COVID-19 pandemic of 2020 and 2021 showed us that life is short. We do not know when our time will come, and at the end of the day, we owe it to ourselves to lose the pretenses, stop trying to please others, and most importantly, reject the idea that who we really are is anything less than the people beside us.

Simply put, authenticity boosts self-confidence, emotional well-being, relationship quality, and overall happiness. A study published in *The Journal of Psychology* found that participants who scored higher in authentic living reported greater happiness, higher self-esteem, better relationships, and more positive emotions than participants who had reported being less authentic (Wood et al., 2008).

You can think about it from a leadership perspective as well. Being a professional is dull sometimes. But when you lead authentically, it spices things up and makes the workplace a more enjoyable and productive environment for everyone. When you lead authentically, you bring your true self and you inspire others to do the same. When you lead authentically, it fosters creativity, encourages open communication, and helps build trust within your team. So, let's ditch the stiff corporate façade and embrace the power of authenticity in our leadership styles. It's time to let our personalities shine and make work a little less dull.

But before we dive deeper, let's start with some basic definitions to ensure we're on the same page. Authenticity is defined as "the quality of being authentic." Authentic is defined as "of undisputed origin; genuine." I define authenticity as "being uniquely you." Your gifts, your unique way of doing things, your goals, your interests, your background, your experiences, and how you show up in life are all uniquely "you" and have brought you to where you are today. And the world deserves to know who you are.

In the work that I do—whether it's speaking, coaching, consulting, teaching, or facilitating—I talk endlessly about self-awareness and knowing who we are. Before we can make changes in our lives, we must first become self-aware of how we are currently showing up. Sometimes, being honest about it is challenging, but doing so is a critical first step. Cultivating authenticity means actively deciding who you want to be rather than settling for who you think others expect you to be. In fact, Cultivate is the first pillar in my C.R.E.A.T.E.^SM Framework:

- **C — Cultivate**: Leadership begins within. Cultivate self-awareness, growth, and the courage to lead from purpose rather than perfection.
- **R — Respect**: Respect yourself first, then extend that respect to others. Listen deeply, honor differences, and model empathy in action.
- **E — Empower**: Empower others by giving them space, trust, and tools to rise. True empowerment builds confidence and multiplies leadership.
- **A — Acknowledge**: Recognition fuels connection. Acknowledge effort, progress, and humanity—both yours and those around you. Gratitude transforms culture.
- **T — Transform**: Change begins when awareness meets action. Transform challenges into lessons and fear into forward motion.
- **E — Engage**: Engagement is leadership in motion. Show up, stay curious, and create environments where people feel seen, heard, and valued.

I wrote this book because authenticity is a necessity; our very lives depend on it. Most of us want to talk about it because we hear the word often, but we still shy away from showing up as our authentic selves. And that's not fair to you or those around you. Everyone has a gift. Everyone has a story. Everyone deserves to show up as they are, without a mask.

This book is for anyone who wants to tap into the power of authenticity and unlock the potential of their true selves. Authenticity is a potent tool to help you become more successful, fulfill your dreams, and explore new opportunities. It's time to commit to living and leading authentically. Because your true self deserves it. This book will show you how to overcome fear and doubt, be genuine in every interaction, and harness the power of authenticity to transform your life. Through personal stories and practical tips, you'll learn how to become an authentic leader and unlock the secrets of living true to yourself. At the end of each chapter, you'll find a section where you can reflect on the topics we've covered and make a plan to take action. Because a goal without a plan is just a wish.

I am unapologetically me and authentically showing up—from here on out. And by the end of this book, I hope you know that you can do the same—and *not* apologize for it. You can say, "I am authentically [insert YOUR name], and I don't apologize for it. I am unapologetically [insert YOUR name]!"

It's time to unleash your inner truth and discover freedom through genuineness. So what do you say: are you ready to start genuinely showing up as yourself every day?

If so, let's get started!

ACTION CHANGES THINGS

Reflect: How does authenticity show up for you?

1. Write your definition of authenticity—no Googling, just you!
2. List two recent situations: one where you felt genuinely authentic and one where you didn't.
3. Reflect on the difference between these two situations:
   - Why did you feel authentic in one scenario and not the other?
   - What pressures or expectations influenced you?
   - What's one simple step you could take to show up more authentically?

Quick Win: Commit to one small action to show up more authentically. Write it down and hold yourself accountable!

"Authenticity is the key to living a life free from regret. And the good news? It's never too late to start." —Paula R Jenkins

NOTES

1

Unapologetically Me

"Leadership isn't just something I teach; it's something that taught me." —Paula R Jenkins

Let's rewind for a minute. Before I ever became a coach, consultant, speaker, or facilitator, I was just … Paula. A young Black woman trying to figure out how to lead, live, and not lose herself in the process.

You've already heard me say that authenticity is essential. It's power. It's your most valuable leadership tool. But let me be clear: I didn't arrive at that belief by reading a leadership book or watching a TED Talk.

Nope. I learned it by surviving the mess, navigating microaggressions, building teams that didn't trust me (at first), and crying in HR before I had to fire someone for the first time.

This chapter focuses on my backstory—the messy, hard, human journey that taught me what authentic leadership looks like—and why I do the work I do today.

Let's Ground This in Reality

What we're told about ourselves—especially early in life—has more power than we realize.

Sociologist Howard Becker introduced something called *Labeling Theory*, which explains how the labels we are given can shape how we see ourselves and how we behave over time.

So when a child is repeatedly called:

"too much"
"too quiet"
"difficult"
"bossy"

Those words don't just pass through.
They stick.
They settle in.
And over time, people start to live in alignment with those labels—whether they are true or not.
That means the way you show up today... may not actually be who you are.
It may be who you were told to be.
And if we're not careful, we carry those labels into adulthood—into our careers, our relationships, our leadership.
We shrink where we were told to be quiet.
We overcompensate where we were told we weren't enough.
We perform where we were never taught to just be.
So when we talk about authenticity...
We're not just talking about "being yourself."
We're talking about **unlearning everything that told you not to.**
This is why authenticity isn't as simple as people make it sound.
The research is clear—this isn't just personal, it's universal.

Childhood Labels & Complexes

Do you have experiences in your childhood that make you cringe, whether it is something someone said or did to you? Or maybe something you said or did to someone? While some of these experiences may seem insignificant, they can change the trajectory of who you are and impact how you appear in the world. I am no different; I have them too. Some I will never speak of because of the pain they bring, and some you will learn about in this book. Just know that your experiences—good or bad—help make you who you are, and your truth should be lived in.

My story is uniquely mine, but it may resonate with some as familiar.

I grew up in a two-parent middle-class home on the south side of Chicago with a younger brother. I went to Montessori School from preschool to second grade, then I went to Catholic school until eighth grade. I was a smart kid who got A's and had friends. I sported the classic '80s starter kit: thick glasses, shiny braces, and all the confidence of someone oblivious to fashion. But I also developed a Napoleon complex during that stage of my life. I was 4'11" for *five* years—yes, five. Trust me, that's plenty of time to perfect your death stare. During this time, I embraced a mindset that I think still defines me today: "Don't mess with me, or I will come for you."

As a result, I was called bossy for many years. I heard it, didn't care, and held an attitude that I was bossy! It is striking how the same characteristics earn girls labels while boys receive compliments. Back in 2014, there was a push to ban the word bossy for girls because it has been shown that girls are labeled as "bossy" and boys are labeled as "leaders." Well, we know the impact this can have on children. And this also shows up in adulthood—I will speak to this later.

As a child, I certainly didn't think about or even understand what "unapologetically being me" meant, let alone "authenticity." I just knew I was me—that's it. I couldn't give anyone anything more or less. I also began to gain weight around age seven or eight. But I showed up confidently in all that I did. Why? Because I was brilliant, and you could NOT tell me anything—seriously.

It was more difficult to maintain that unapologetic authenticity in high school.

I went to Whitney M. Young Magnet (WY) High School. At the time, it was the best public high school in Chicago and one of the best in the nation. You had to take a test to get into this school. I remember thinking I would attend a Catholic high school since I was already on that track, but I applied to WY and got in. Go Dolphins! But, needless to say, I was surrounded by brilliant minds, and I questioned if I belonged. I often quieted myself because, at times, I didn't feel like I fit in. Even though I met lifelong friends that I still speak to today, high school did not allow me to show up as my true self in all senses.

However, things did get better quickly when I found what I was great at—singing. I spent four years in the concert choir, and it was a breath of fresh air, truly one of the highlights of high school. I took an honors physics class and found that I was not only good at it, but I also really enjoyed it. I also took an English class that brought out my true love of reading, which still exists today. I was excited by assignments in English that challenged students to read as many books as possible. I was that student who not only did it but exceeded any expectations.

This helped me begin the process of finding who I was and what I enjoyed—bringing me to the next phase of my life.

College: Finding My Voice

When I first stepped foot on Tuskegee University's campus, an unapologetic and authentic Paula made her appearance once again (HBCU love for life!). I found my voice. I showed up, and I swear I never looked back. Your environment—especially as a young adult—can bring out characteristics that never appeared in your early childhood or high school years. This can be based on circumstances, the people you surround yourself with, or experiences—good and bad.

My experiences in college allowed me to show up as a leader many times—not always the best leader, but a leader nonetheless. As the Chicago Club President, I had opportunities to speak to the college president, faculty, and teachers across campus. This role allowed me to provide support and representation for a group of students who were immediately judged based on where they were from (does that resonate with anyone?). As a leader, it can be challenging to show up during hardships and advocate for those around you especially as you are being held to a different standard. But the beauty of authenticity is finding your voice and standing up for what's right, regardless.

In college, many of us strive to gain approval from our peers and mentors, often causing us to overthink and second-guess ourselves. This can make authenticity feel difficult to maintain, heightening its importance for leaders. You can create meaningful connections and impactful change by being honest with yourself about your strengths and weaknesses, embracing your unique gifts and sharing them with others, and taking risks to make a difference in the college community. Being authentic is necessary not only for successful leadership in college but also for fostering personal growth and development that will carry through into adulthood. With authenticity as your guide, you can confidently lead the way to becoming an inspiring leader who makes a difference.

I held on to this mindset throughout my college career, which proved well for me as I transitioned to adulthood. For any college student reading this book, I want to cheer you on to follow your heart, embrace what excites you, and speak up; later in life, you will be glad you did!

Early Career & Hard Lessons

Early adulthood brings you into a space of choosing how you show up; you are now in the "real world!" So, how on Earth do you show up as your authentic self?

I am a long way off from being a young adult, but I still remember trying to determine how to show up, as my years right out of college were rocky. I had multiple job offers after graduation as a Computer Information Systems major. I chose a job as a programmer based primarily on location rather than the job or opportunity itself—a big mistake. I found myself out of a job within three months and then had to work two to three jobs to make ends meet (in my opinion, not worthy of a CIS major in the mid-90s!). I moved back home and worked for my extended family for four years in a role that allowed me to manage operations for multiple restaurants, but I found myself working alone. I quickly realized that this extrovert could not sustainably function in this type of job.

During those four years, I recognized that I was not showing up as my authentic self, and I, indeed, was not being intentional about living or leading in such a way. This led to the first onset of depression I experienced. When you have high expectations for yourself, and those around you do too, it is hard to show up for yourself and be your true self, especially without understanding how you even got to that point.

At that time, I reconnected with a high school friend; we began dating and eventually got married. As I started my new life as a married woman, I decided I would quit my job and start my search for a new career. Well, let's just say, that was not a fun time. I was not happy. I was frustrated and frankly, mean. It took me months to find a new job. And once I did, I knew it still wasn't what I should be doing, but it was an "in" for the company I wanted to work at. I kept thinking, *Is this the life I want? Am I being true to myself?*

Finding the "right" job can be tricky, but sometimes, we end up in a job that isn't quite the perfect fit but with a company we believe in. In these situations, putting on a façade and trying to make the job work can be tempting, but showing up authentically is crucial. Being true to yourself and your needs allows you to be more productive and enables the company to understand where you excel and where you may need more support. It's essential to have open and honest conversations with your manager and team about your strengths, weaknesses, and career goals. This way, you can work together to find a role within the company that suits you better. If that's not possible, then it's better to be honest about your needs and find a job that aligns with them rather than stay in a job where you cannot be your authentic self.

This was critical for me as I knew from the moment I joined the company that I wanted to grow quickly and move into a role that would use my skillset to everyone's benefit. I also stated my intentions clearly: I wanted to leave the role within a year. I know that my direct nature was a part of this conversation, but I also needed to be true to myself and show up honestly with my manager. For the record: I *was* promoted within a year!

To my young adult readers, being authentic is not just a buzzword; it's a way of life, especially as a young professional. When we're true to ourselves, we're not only happier and fulfilled, but it also helps us to be more successful in our careers. Authenticity inspires creativity, open communication, and trust within the workplace. So, let's stop pretending to be someone else and let our passions and personalities shine. Society may have a mold for us, but let's break free and live authentically. It's time to embrace our quirks and unique perspectives and live on our terms. Trust me, you won't regret it. Being unapologetic isn't about arrogance; it's about acceptance. Be unapologetically you.

One of the things I learned throughout my young adulthood is that it is so important to show up. This does not mean that every decision I made was the right one or that I lived a perfect life, but it does mean that I focused on being who I was and didn't have the energy to do anything different. Authenticity doesn't mean you stop improving; it means you start embracing who you are while doing it.

Why I Choose to Lead with Heart

My early years in corporate America were filled with being clear, direct, and intentional about what I wanted to do. I was hired by an HR company, thinking I could get into HR which was my goal at the time. Instead, several others and I were hired to answer pension calls in a call center. As a group of highly educated professionals, we were immediately looking at each other, trying to figure out how we ended up here. There we were, bright-eyed graduates, degrees in hand, answering pension questions we barely understood. Talk about humble beginnings! I knew it would just be temporary for me, but I had to make my career goals and desires clear.

Even still, I learned the importance of being my authentic self early on, but I also quickly recognized that doing so would put me in positions that were uncomfortable for others because they were not used to "people like me." I vividly remember a young woman who started with me at the call center stating that she had never met a Black person before. She went on to say that where she was from, she only saw Black people on TV. Well, let's say that told me all I needed to know. Historically, the way Black people have been portrayed on TV has been less than kind. She also mentioned how she loved my "sassiness." Now, I didn't take that as a compliment, but I quickly recognized where she was coming from and that I was showing up as me, at all times.

This encounter made me realize that even though I grew up on the south side of Chicago, I had been exposed to people of all kinds during my short twenty-five years. On the flip side, it also made me realize that many people have not been, and their views of me and others were based on that lack of exposure. This interaction helped me understand the importance of leading authentically from the beginning of my career.

After my time at the call center, I went on to become an analyst and remained focused on the next role. As time went on, I climbed the corporate ladder, getting promoted often and eventually leading a team as a people manager. This is where my passion for leadership began, and before long, it showed up in everything I did. The number of my peers in leadership who didn't care about their people, didn't understand that we all can grow, and weren't interested in being better leaders shocked me. I also learned that as a Black woman manager, I was looked at differently, and my direct style of leading was on display and subject to review and criticism.

The first time I had to fire a direct report, it broke me. In that moment, it didn't matter to me that they deserved to be fired because they were not performing their job at the expected level. It hurt me because I was taking someone's paycheck away, and I can't say I liked that feeling. I cried so much firing my first employee, I think HR questioned if they'd accidentally fired me instead.

However, I learned a lesson that day that I'll never forget. As I prepared for the meeting, I was getting emotional, and a senior manager approached me. She told me, "Your emotions are okay. When you get to a point where you can fire someone without feeling anything, it is time for you to stop managing people." I will never forget those words because they meant that my authentic self—the person who was showing up—was valid for feeling the way I did. Trust me, if firing someone ever becomes easy, you've officially become the villain in someone else's story! I was a caring manager who knew I had a job but also felt terrible for the employee. I have kept those words close to me for over twenty-five years—and yes, I've had to fire others over the years, and every time, I cared about the well-being of the person whose job was being taken away. That is who I am. One of the key characteristics that I find most important in leaders is empathy; without it, you lack the basics of leadership.

As I moved through my career over the years, I encountered many examples of what leading authentically looked like and what it didn't. The years went by, and I managed teams of two, four, ten, twenty, etc. The number of direct reports I had didn't matter; what mattered was that I showed up as a caring manager who got the job done. This—like leading teams—was not always easy. Regardless, we must recognize the role that we have, and we must not be selfish in our role but instead identify how we can lead in the best way for our current team. And that means letting go of our ego and our own needs to serve the team and company better.

A powerful example of this is when I led a team of seventeen direct reports at a new company, and I immediately knew there was a lack of trust because of their prior managers. They certainly didn't trust me and didn't want to get to know me. Within two months of starting, I knew I had to do something drastic, so I did. I asked the team in an anonymous survey to answer two questions, but instead, I made it personal. I asked: What am I doing well as a manager? And what could I be doing better as a manager? I knew it was critical to get these answers because our clients' success depended upon it.

Once I got the feedback, I collated the data into two documents—one with all the answers to what I was doing well and one with all the answers to what I could be doing better. Then, in our team meeting, I passed out copies of both to every team member. There was silence in the room. I knew they were thinking, *Is she crazy?* And my answer, as I said it out loud, was: "No, I am not crazy! But I do want you to know I believe in feedback, and we must create a culture where we can speak freely, and that all starts with me."

While the feedback on what I did well was excellent, I would be lying if I said a few of the comments on the improvement document didn't hit hard. Reading their constructive criticism was like looking in a funhouse mirror—not pretty but impossible to ignore. But I didn't shy away from them. Instead, I told the team I would work on them. This one meeting was a game changer for our team. After that challenging conversation, we worked better together, and communication was more transparent and honest. Yes, I took one for the team, but showing that I could be vulnerable was important, and it made a huge difference. Leading can be hard, but it can also be pretty gratifying when we focus on being intentionally authentic with our teams.

I didn't learn how to lead authentically from a textbook; I learned it in the trenches. I learned it while being underestimated, mislabeled, overlooked, and challenged at every turn. But through it all, I chose to keep showing up as me. While anything else would've been easier, it wouldn't have been honest.

My leadership journey wasn't about perfection; it was about presence. It was about people. It was about doing the hard thing with heart. That's what makes leadership real. And that's what I'm inviting you to do too.

Adult Life & Intentional Authenticity

Now that I am well into my career, I have come to recognize that my authenticity is what I owe myself, as well as those around me, at all times. Please don't get me wrong: this does not mean everything I think comes out of my mouth. We still must be careful with our language. I always think back to the quote about how "our thoughts become words, words become actions, actions become habits, habits become character, and character becomes your destiny." Everything we think doesn't have to be shared. Seriously.

I am in a space of desiring joy, happiness, and peace around me. I choose to bring this into my life; otherwise, I don't allow it. It's essential to be intentional about how you do so in living and leading an authentically fulfilling life. This means saying goodbye to people, organizations, things, and places that don't honor where you are in your current space. Letting go can be difficult, but it is often necessary to be true to yourself and live authentically.

For a long time, I held on to things that no longer served me. Toxic relationships, hostile environments, or even material possessions can hold us back from reaching our full potential. It's essential to take a step back, evaluate what is truly important to us, and let go of anything that doesn't align with our values and goals. It's okay to say goodbye to people and things that are not good for us, even if it hurts in the moment. It's important to prioritize our well-being and happiness. It's not always an easy process, but it is necessary for living an authentic life. Don't shrink to fit places you've outgrown. Remember, letting go is not the end of the world; it's the beginning of a new one where you can truly be yourself. I'm doing it, and it feels GOOD!

I have chosen to be who I am personally and professionally without apology to ensure that I show up as best I can, as often as I can. This is not easy, and it is far easier in my personal life than in my professional life. But the fact that I know this, can state it, and am working on it makes me authentic in recognizing I still need to grow and learn. This mindset is essential to this process.

Let's take a minute to reflect.

Do you know who you are? Knowing who you are authentically in your personal life is a powerful and transformative experience. Authenticity encourages self-awareness, improves your relationships, and gives you the strength to make decisions that reflect who you truly are. This exploration will enable you to find authenticity in yourself and build up your confidence. By embracing authenticity, your relationships can be built on a solid foundation of trust and understanding, leading to meaningful communication and deeper connections with those around you.

Knowing who you are authentically in your professional life is essential for success. Authenticity in the workplace allows you to own up to mistakes, show vulnerability, and build trust with colleagues. This will create an honest and transparent environment for growth and collaboration. By embracing who you are, you are showing your team members that you are approachable, trustworthy, and understanding. Your authenticity will lead to more effective leadership and higher morale among your team members. Finally, it will allow you to make decisions that reflect your values and goals and create a work culture that reflects who you are and what you believe in. This authenticity will lead to a more meaningful and successful career.

As an entrepreneur, I have found myself in spaces and places where I have questioned whether I belong and whether I have what it takes. This has been humbling and has cost me years of growth. But we must continually recognize where we need to grow and learn because we will only know if we speak it.

Every phase in my journey taught me something crucial: authenticity doesn't happen by accident; it must be intentionally cultivated, one choice at a time.

ACTION CHANGES THINGS

Reflect: What is your leadership story? Note: Leadership is not about a title; you can lead from any seat.

1. Think back to the first time you led someone. What was happening? How did you feel?
2. What is one moment you're proud of as a leader? What made it authentic?
3. Now think about a moment where you didn't lead the way you wanted to. Why not? What would you do differently now?
4. What values have guided your leadership journey? Are you still leading by them today?

Quick Win: Choose one guiding value. Schedule a 15-minute task that visibly demonstrates it (e.g., mentor check-in, feedback round, clear decision).

"I'd rather be questioned for being real than praised for playing a role." —Paula R Jenkins

NOTES

2

Leading with Authenticity

"Authenticity is your most precious commodity as a leader." — commonly attributed to Marcus Buckingham

Would you trust a leader who doesn't even trust themselves? Probably not, right?

That's because leading with authenticity starts at the top, and it's about being true to yourself and your values while fostering an environment of trust and respect among your team members.

So, how do you lead with authenticity?

The first step is understanding and communicating your leadership style. Start by taking a simple leadership assessment online or reflecting on the characteristics you naturally exhibit when leading others.

Here are several well-known leadership styles to consider:

1. **Servant Leader:** Prioritizes serving others, empowering the team, and fostering collaboration.
2. **Transformational Leader:** Inspires and motivates the team to achieve ambitious goals through a compelling vision.
3. **Democratic Leader:** Encourages team input, values diverse perspectives, and fosters group decision-making.
4. **Autocratic Leader:** Makes decisions independently, providing clear directions and expectations.

5. **Laissez-faire Leader:** Offers autonomy to team members, allowing them to self-direct with minimal supervision.
6. **Coaching Leader:** Focuses on developing team members' individual strengths, providing ongoing mentorship and feedback.

Ask yourself what you value most as a leader: Is it prioritizing teamwork or encouraging autonomy and independence? Are you focused on inspiring your team or developing their individual strengths? Do you prefer efficiency or more democratic decision-making?

Next, you must become familiar with your strengths and weaknesses, while also being open to feedback and growth. By understanding yourself, you will be better equipped to lead in a way that aligns with your values and goals.

As a leader, every time I am on a new team or in a new organization, I have made it a point to inform those around me of my leadership style. I am a direct communicator and a servant leader. I share in advance that I want to get to know them each personally, and they can share what they are comfortable with when we meet. This goes a long way when leading. Over the years, I have had numerous people tell me that they have never had a manager even ask about them personally or take the time to get to know them. It may seem like a small gesture, but it matters. You can't lead effectively if you're busy pretending to be someone else.

"Good Morning" — The Power of What Seems Small

01 THE SITUATION
Early in my journey as a people manager, I was assigned a new team. I was still getting to know everyone and figuring out how to show up for them as their leader.

02 THE CHALLENGE
At the time, I didn't think I was doing anything extraordinary. I was simply showing up as myself — greeting people, engaging, and being present. What I didn't realize was that what felt "normal" to me was not normal for everyone else.

03 THE TURNING POINT
A few weeks in, one of my direct reports said, "I want to thank you for being a great manager." When I asked why, he said: "You come in every morning and say 'Good morning,' and I want to thank you for that." I had no idea that felt significant.

04 THE REALITY CHECK
He told me his previous manager sat in the exact same seat for years and never once said good morning. Not once. Two words — that's all it took to make his day.

05 THE AUTHENTIC SHIFT
In that moment, I realized: what we think is "normal" isn't normal for everyone. We all experience leadership differently. What feels small to you can mean everything to someone else. I wasn't doing anything special — I was just being me.

06 THE RESULT
That interaction shifted how I viewed leadership forever. Authenticity isn't always about big, bold moments. Sometimes it's about the small, consistent behaviors that show people they matter.

> **Authenticity without awareness can still create disconnect. Authenticity with intention builds trust.**

REFLECT

1. What do you do daily that you think is "normal" — but might actually be meaningful to someone else?
2. How do you acknowledge the people around you?
3. Are you creating connection… or just co-existing?

ACT — THIS WEEK

- Greet people by name every morning.
- Make intentional eye contact and engage.
- Thank someone specifically for something they've done.

Don't overthink it. Just do it. Because sometimes, two simple words can change someone's entire day.

Let's Ground This in Reality

If you think that story was just a 'nice moment'—it's not. Research backs this up.

Authenticity in leadership isn't just a "nice to have." It directly impacts how people show up, how they perform, and whether they trust you at all.

Research on authentic leadership by Fred Walumbwa and his colleagues found that leaders who are self-aware, transparent, and aligned with their values create stronger, more effective teams. These leaders build higher levels of trust, increase employee engagement, and improve overall job satisfaction.

In other words…

When people believe you are real—they respond differently.

And it doesn't stop there.

Harvard researcher Amy Edmondson introduced the concept of psychological safety, showing that teams perform best when people feel safe to speak openly—without fear of embarrassment or punishment.

Think about that for a second.

If your team doesn't feel safe to speak up...

> they're not giving you their best ideas.
> they're not challenging decisions.
> they're not fully showing up.

That's not a people problem.

That's a leadership environment problem.

So let's bring this back to you.

Psychologist Daniel Goleman's work on emotional intelligence shows that leadership success is not driven by IQ or technical skills alone. It's driven by a leader's ability to understand themselves, manage their emotions, and respond effectively to others.

And here's where it all connects:

Authenticity and emotional intelligence go hand in hand.

Because you cannot lead authentically if you are not aware of how you show up and how people experience you.

So when we talk about leading with authenticity...

We're not just talking about being "nice" or "approachable."

We're talking about:

- building trust
- creating safe environments
- understanding your impact
- and showing up in a way that allows others to do the same

Because leadership is not just about what you say.

It's about what people experience when they're around you. So this isn't just about being 'good leader.' It's about being an effective one.

The Power of Open Communication

Another critical aspect of leading authentically is fostering open communication within your team. This means encouraging team members to share their thoughts, ideas, and concerns while also actively listening to what they say. When team members feel their voices are heard, they are more likely to be engaged and motivated. Additionally, it's essential to lead by example and be transparent in your communication and actions; this will help you build trust and earn respect from your team members.

Open communication is critical because you can only learn what's happening in an environment that allows honesty. Over the years, I have done various things to build trust. When I have a new team, one of the first things I do is ask each person separately two simple questions: What is going well? And what could be better? These questions can open a door of pure gold, revealing things you'd never have known without asking directly.

Now, I know what you're thinking: *Sounds good, but people won't always be honest.* And that's true—unless you intentionally create a culture where honesty is welcomed without judgment or consequences. If people fear retaliation, silence will always win.

Here are a few practical ways to foster this kind of trust and open communication:

- **Set the tone early.** Start meetings with quick check-ins that humanize the space and invite real conversation.
- **Be consistent.** Trust builds over time. Don't just ask for feedback once and disappear.
- **Follow up.** If someone shares something, circle back and show you heard them, whether you act on it or not.
- **Model it.** Share your lessons learned, mistakes, and leadership blind spots. Vulnerability invites vulnerability.
- **Make it safe.** Be crystal clear that feedback—especially constructive feedback—won't lead to punishment.

People will be honest when they feel safe, seen, and supported. And that's on you as the leader to cultivate. Remember the 'C' in the C.R.E.A.T.E.^{SM} Framework? If you're doing it right, then you won't have to chase the truth; it'll find you. I won't go into the full framework in this book, but please check out the resources in the QR code at the end of this book.

Integrity: Being True to Your Values

Leading authentically means being true to your values and leading with integrity. The standard definition of integrity is "the quality of being honest and having strong moral principles; moral uprightness." But integrity is more than a definition; it's a daily decision. It's showing up when it's hard, telling the truth when it's uncomfortable, and doing the right thing when no one's watching.

Leading with integrity means being honest and transparent in your actions and decisions and holding yourself and your team members accountable. It's also about consistency—being the same person in every room and standing up for your beliefs, even if they're unpopular. That kind of leadership creates a culture of trust and respect, where collaboration and productivity thrive.

"I have never met a Black woman who can say what you say and keep their job!" That's what another Black woman told me years ago in corporate America. At first, I laughed and said, "Well, I do my job well, and my clients and team don't seem to have an issue with my style." But I quickly understood what she meant: she was referring to how I spoke truth to power. The reality is, I didn't—and still don't—know how to be anything but myself. Authentically, unapologetically Paula. But how did I get there, especially in a work setting? It started with identifying my values. So, how do you identify yours?

Start by asking yourself:

- What principles guide my decision-making, even when it's tough?

- What am I willing to walk away from if it means compromising something important to me?
- Who are the people I admire most, and what values do they represent?
- When have I felt most proud of myself—and why?

Your values often show up in moments of tension, when you're forced to choose between what's easy and what's right. That's where integrity lives. For example:

- If **honesty** is a core value, it means you don't sugarcoat the truth, even when it's awkward.
- If **respect** is your value, you don't allow side conversations in meetings or tolerate eye-rolls when someone is speaking.
- If you value **accountability**, you own your mistakes (and expect your team to do the same).
- If **equity** matters to you, you speak up when others are left out—even if it puts your comfort at risk.

Defining your values gives you a filter for how to lead, and living them gives your team a reason to trust you. I conduct a values exercise in many of my emotional quotient (EQ) workshops. EQ, much like IQ, is a way to measure emotional intelligence, which is the ability to perceive, understand, manage, and use one's own emotions and the emotions of others (Murtoff, 2025). You can access that resource by scanning the QR code at the end of this book.

Leading authentically embodies the 'R' in my C.R.E.A.T.E.[SM] Framework: Respect. Authentic leaders respect themselves, their team's potential, and the responsibilities they hold. Leading authentically also directly aligns with 'E' for Empower in my C.R.E.A.T.E.[SM] Framework. Authentic leaders empower their teams by creating a safe space for honesty, vulnerability, and growth.

Recognizing Inauthentic Leadership

My final year of leading in corporate America was one of the most challenging years for me to date. While it is important to present yourself as a strong and capable leader, we must also understand that leading with authenticity means opening up about our concerns and worries to our direct reports. When we don't provide transparency to our teams, we lose valuable time and people because we can't be honest about what is needed. We become inauthentic leaders.

And lacking transparency is only one example of being an inauthentic leader.

Leaders who take credit for the work of others, make false promises, or engage in unethical behavior are inauthentic. These are leaders who might be charismatic on the surface but lack authenticity and integrity in their actions. Other examples include leaders who use fear tactics to motivate employees, manipulate situations for personal gain, or fail to take responsibility for their shortcomings.

Here are some specific instances I've witnessed or discussed with my clients:

- A leader advocating for diversity but failing to address discrimination internally.
- A leader publicly humiliates team members to boost their image.
- A leader sets impossible expectations without providing necessary support.
- A political leader who publicly advocates for specific policies but privately works against them for personal gain.
- A leader who claims to have an open-door policy but is not accessible or responsive to their team members.

These examples illustrate how a leader who is not leading authentically can create a hostile work environment and a lack of trust within the team and broader organization as a whole.

When an organization is led by inauthentic leaders, it can create a hostile environment, which is defined as a workplace that makes employees feel "uncomfortable, scared, or intimidated" due to unwelcome conduct. I have had clients tell me about situations that have impacted them so deeply that they have, in the words of our current culture, begun to quit quietly. The quiet quitting phenomenon is defined as doing the minimum requirements of one's job and putting in no more time, effort, or enthusiasm than necessary. Here are some of their stories:

- The manager sends an urgent email after 5:00 p.m. then follows up at 7:00 a.m. about no action being taken, but they have yet to call or reach out to their direct report about the urgent matter.
- The manager yells at a subordinate. This is *never* okay; we are all adults and deserve to be treated with respect.
- The manager has not had a 1:1 meeting with the employee all year but during the employee's annual review, has a litany of "issues" to go over and gives the employee a poor rating. In other words, the manager in this case is blindsiding the employee.
- The manager promotes an employee who is not ready for a new role and is not given the appropriate guidance or coaching before starting the new role. A new manager is hired and is told that this employee is not capable of running projects. This new manager is taken aback, given that they know the employee was promoted months prior. This has now led to a lack of confidence in this employee, and everyone knows it except the employee and the new manager.
- The manager provides new opportunities to one team member consistently. The other members on the team don't understand why they aren't getting new opportunities. The employee requests feedback and requests 1:1s to address their concerns. The manager does not make time for this employee until the annual review.

This type of leadership is dangerous and disengages your employees. If you found yourself cringing at what you read in any of the above examples, I want you to pause and take stock of why you behaved this way. I want you to take a moment and think about when you did this, whom you did it to, and how you can ensure this behavior doesn't occur going forward. I want you to own this behavior and even take it a step further—an action step right now. Take the time to apologize. Own it. While an apology won't fix what happened, it still tells the receiver that you recognize the behavior was wrong and want to inform them that you are at least aware.

Authenticity in Volunteer Leadership

Up to this point, I have talked about leading in a work setting, which is critical, but there is another part of leading that is just as important: leading in a volunteer capacity.

Being a volunteer leader is a unique opportunity to make a difference in the community and the lives of those you work with daily. And what better way to do that than by leading with authenticity? When you bring your true self, you inspire others to do the same by creating a positive and productive environment. Embracing your unique personality can make the volunteer experience more enjoyable for everyone.

In volunteer roles, authenticity is even more critical than it is in a professional environment. People show up because they believe in a cause, not because they need a paycheck. Therefore, the authenticity you bring—or don't bring—often determines whether they stay or quietly disappear.

I have led various organizations as a volunteer, and it has been rewarding but also challenging. I remember being challenged by a member of the organization about "what I should be doing in my role," and I quickly realized the member was uneducated on policies and procedures. I initially took issue with the language being used but remembered that sometimes members, especially in non-profit organizations, won't always have the same knowledge, care, or commitment that you do. This can be challenging for those leading. In this scenario, I reminded the member of the rules and what my role entailed in terms of what I could and couldn't do. While the lesson here is making sure your members are informed, you have to remember that everyone won't be aligned, and it's your role to educate when challenged, not to make the situation worse by taking it personally.

Leading Without a Paycheck

Have you ever experienced that feeling when you are volunteering, doing what you love or have a passion for, and you know you aren't getting paid, but there is that sinking feeling of questioning yourself? It can be daunting when you attend the meetings, lead them, take the abuse, don't get the thank yous, get excessive text messages, emails, phone calls, etc. This takes exceptional patience, love for what you are doing, and authenticity.

Here are some examples that, as a volunteer leader, you have experienced or probably will experience along with solutions for how to handle:

- **Uninformed members:** Lead through education, not confrontation.
- **Late-night emergencies:** Set clear boundaries and offer alternative ways to find information.
- **Public confrontations:** Keep calm, redirect conversations, and avoid taking things personally.

This is what comes with leading in a volunteer role sometimes. It's not fun, but it comes with the territory. You can manage this and lead with authenticity by setting boundaries, continuously helping those in your organization understand the rules, and finally, removing yourself from any organization that is not serving you well. This last one is important because you can't lead well if it brings you anxiety and frustration or limits you from having a positive impact in your role.

The key is knowing that your transparency, vulnerability, and authenticity are still important as a leader even when there is no monetary compensation. I would argue this point even more in a volunteer role because those around you and your organization can decide to leave at any time. Accept the role that you have and the roles of others. If it works, then continue to lead; if it doesn't, you have to do what's best for you. Everyone around you may not understand, and sometimes, it's not for you to explain. People will always have an opinion about your decision, but they are usually the last to step up to help. Your authenticity in volunteer roles is essential because it lets those around you know they are not alone.

I remember having a board meeting with a group at the height of the COVID-19 pandemic, and I broke down and cried hard. I had never done this on any call, but I was not in a good place and had to be honest, vulnerable, and transparent. I even apologized for doing so but recognized that I was in a safe space—one where I needed them to know what I was experiencing. The number of board members who reached out and said, "Thank you," to me was mind-blowing. To this day, I am grateful to them for wrapping their arms around me but, more importantly, for allowing me a safe space and stating that my authenticity made them feel less alone. It also showed that I was human. Let me say that again: it showed that I was human. Too often, we show up trying to handle it all, but there are times when we must take the superwoman/man cape off. Period.

Even during those challenging leadership roles that feel thankless, I want to take a moment and state how important it is to surround yourself with people who will challenge you and not be "yes people." In every organization I have led, I have been blessed to have team members who challenged me, coached me, and had my back every time. This is important because we need to be corrected, and you must have people question you to ensure you are leading your team or organization effectively.

Final Thoughts: Communicating Authentically Everywhere

I want to end this chapter by saying that many leaders who lead organizations for their careers also lead in nonprofit organizations. Sometimes, you show up the same in both places, and sometimes, you don't. This can be represented in how you communicate with people—your tone, your attitude, your body language, your written messages, etc. Everything begins and ends with communication. This is so important to understand because whether you are in your professional job, your volunteer organization, or even just your day-to-day conversations, how you show up reflects on your ability to work with and converse with people. The words we use matter. The amount of attention we show someone who is speaking matters. The body language we show matters. Take the time to remind yourself of how you would want to be treated in these situations.

Regardless of where you are showing up to lead, my request is that you show up as you. Great leaders aren't perfect; they're authentic.

ACTION CHANGES THINGS

Reflect: How are my core values showing up in my leadership?

1. **List your top 3 core values** (e.g., Integrity, Respect, Empathy):
2. **Evaluate your leadership roles** (paid & volunteer). Do your current actions match these core values?
   YES | NO (circle one)
3. If **NO**, write down one step you can take to better realign your leadership with your core values:

Quick Win: Tell one person (a colleague, team member, or friend) what you're working on. Accountability leads to alignment.

"Authenticity isn't optional; it's essential. Your team deserves the real you." —Paula R Jenkins

NOTES

3

Living Authentically

"Be yourself; everyone else is taken."

— commonly attributed to Oscar Wilde

Do you know how to be yourself? I mean, *genuinely* be yourself?

I want to spend some time talking about living authentically. Being yourself is the greatest gift you can give yourself and the world. And don't get me wrong: living unapologetically authentic does not mean treating people with disrespect or being unkind. Being unapologetic just means you show up as you are and live in it without feeling like you have to explain who you are—you just are. We all have things about ourselves that we need to work on, but it does not mean we should apologize for who we are.

CHAPTER THREE · LIVING AUTHENTICALLY

What It Feels Like to Not Be Yourself

01 — THE SITUATION

I have worked with many people who will say it plainly: "I'm not living authentically." And if we're honest, most of us can relate. There are areas of our lives where we show up fully — and others where we shrink, adjust, or hide. Not because we want to, but because we feel like we have to.

02 — THE CHALLENGE

When you are not living authentically, it doesn't sit quietly in the background — it shows up. As internal conflict, anxiety, emptiness, dissatisfaction, resentment, anger, and most commonly: fear of rejection. You may look fine on the outside, but internally, something feels off.

03 — WHAT WAS AT STAKE

This isn't just about feelings. It impacts how you lead, how you show up in relationships, how you make decisions, and how you see yourself. Over time, it chips away at your confidence and your sense of self.

04 — THE TURNING POINT

I had a client who struggled with this for most of their life. By the time they came to coaching, it was showing up everywhere — personally and professionally. They wanted confidence, transparency, sincerity, and integrity. But they didn't know how to get there. So we started asking the real questions: What are you protecting? Why are you holding back? What are you afraid will happen if you show up fully?

05 — THE AUTHENTIC SHIFT

The breakthrough came from permission. Permission to stop performing, stop pleasing, and stop filtering themselves for acceptance. And simply be who they already were. Not a new version — the real one.

06 — THE RESULT

Once they allowed themselves to show up as themselves, everything changed. Not overnight — but noticeably. They made different decisions. They showed up with more clarity and confidence. The world didn't change. They did.

Living authentically isn't always about doing something new. Sometimes, it's about letting go of what was never you to begin with.

REFLECT

1. *Where in your life are you not fully showing up as yourself?*
2. *What are you afraid will happen if you do?*
3. *Who are you trying to please — and why?*
4. *What are you protecting?*

ACT — THIS WEEK

Identify one area where you've been holding back. Then ask yourself:

"What would it look like if I showed up as myself here?"

Not perfectly. Not loudly. Just honestly. Because hiding costs more than being seen ever will.

Let's Ground This in Reality

If you think hiding parts of yourself is just "how life works"… it's not. There's a real cost to it.

Code-Switching & Identity Strain

Research shows:
Research highlighted by Harvard Business Review found that many professionals—especially Black employees and people of color—feel pressure to code-switch, adjusting how they speak, behave, and show up to fit workplace norms. While it may help navigate certain environments, this constant self-monitoring leads to emotional exhaustion, stress, and reduced engagement.

Why it matters:
When you feel like you can't be yourself, it doesn't just drain you—it disconnects you.

Authenticity in Relationships

Research shows:
Research by psychologist Harry Reis and his colleagues found that when people feel safe being their true selves, it strengthens trust, emotional connection, and relationship satisfaction. When people feel the need to hide parts of who they are, it creates distance and weakens relationships over time.

Why it matters:
You can't build real relationships if you're not showing up as your real self.

So this isn't just about comfort.
It's about connection, energy, and the life you're actually living.

And if you've ever felt tired from constantly adjusting who you are…

this is why.

Everything Begins and Ends with Communication

I dedicate a whole chapter later in the book to communicating authentically, but I want to address living authentically from a communication perspective.

Let's first define what the word communication means. According to Merriam-Webster, communication is "a process by which information is exchanged between individuals through a common system of symbols, signs, or behavior." In everything we do, we communicate to others who we are and what may or may not be happening. We do this through our body language, facial expressions, words, and more. Likewise, communication style refers to the manner in which we, as individuals, share information with others. There are various models to identify your communication styles, but I prefer and highly recommend the DISC method, which talks about four dominant communication styles.

When we choose to live authentically from a communication perspective, it means being true to ourselves and our values through our interactions with others. It means being honest and transparent in our communication, being aware of our communication style, and adapting our communication style to the needs of the situation. It also means being receptive to feedback, embracing personal growth, and being authentic in our nonverbal communication.

I have found it challenging to live authentically from a communication perspective because I can be terse, direct, and short, especially when I feel customer service isn't up to par. I have learned over the years to temper my reaction, though I am still growing in this area. The goal is to continue to grow and be aware of how I show up (more on that in a later chapter). The point is to focus on doing your best when showing up and learning from your experiences—good and bad.

Being Unapologetic

I have made it a point in my life to be unapologetic about who I am, and in some cases, it has served me very well; in others, not so much. I say this because I want you to understand that there are consequences to how we show up, even when we show up authentically.

Being unapologetically authentic means being true to yourself and your values, no matter what. It's about not compromising who you are or what you stand for to please others. This is important because it allows us to show up as our true selves without feeling ashamed or embarrassed about who we are. It's a form of self-love and acceptance that will enable us to be confident in who we are and what we stand for.

The greatest example of this in our culture, in my opinion, is the singer Lizzo. For those who may be unfamiliar with Lizzo, she is a performer who, in her lyrics, speaks unapologetically about being overweight. I have grown to appreciate who she is and how she shows up, truly unapologetic every time. I know most people will never get to this point. Even still, I can't help but think about how freeing it must be for her to be able to do it at her age and in a society that takes pleasure in demeaning anyone who doesn't meet societal expectations for how a person "should" look. She has given a voice to a forgotten mass of people who show up silently because of how the world views them. Kudos to her and everyone who is showing up now because of her.

Unapologetic authenticity also means being open to feedback from others and learning from our mistakes, but never apologizing if it doesn't feel right or necessary. It's about standing firm in our beliefs and values even when we know others might disagree. Unapologetic authenticity is powerful—so don't be afraid to use it!

Relationships

Living authentically and unapologetically in relationships means being true to yourself and your values while also being respectful of the needs and boundaries of others. It means being honest and transparent in your communication and willing to share your thoughts, feelings, and needs in a healthy way. It also means listening to and understanding the perspectives of others and working together to find solutions that align with both of your values and goals.

At the same time, living authentically also means standing up for yourself and not compromising your values or needs to please others. It means being assertive, setting boundaries, and not being afraid to speak up when something is wrong. Additionally, you should be willing to take responsibility for your actions and own your mistakes instead of blaming others. Remember, you can respect others while still being unapologetic about who you are and what you stand for and not being afraid to show your true self, even if it isn't popular.

Have you ever shown up differently in a romantic relationship to get the other person to like you more? Or do something for you? Most of us have done this at some point in our lives. The issue with this behavior is that it sends the wrong message to our partner and can lead to problems.

You know what I'm talking about: the woman who watches football to appease her mate but is bored out of her mind for three hours (Oh, is that just me?); the man who sits through who knows how many rom-com movies or TV shows, thinking, *Why am I here?* (Thanks, babe!); or the person who constantly changes how they show up in front of their partner's friends in order to keep up some appearance.

While compromise is essential in any romantic relationship, there's a difference in compromise and not being your authentic self. We are doing a disservice to those around us when we put on airs, pretenses, or even completely different personalities. Be you. At all times. Even in your relationships. Inauthenticity is not living, and it certainly does not lead to a healthy relationship. Focus on being your true self and being honest about who you are, what you like, and what brings you joy. This allows for healthy and fulfilling relationships built on trust and mutual respect.

Professional

I know what you're thinking: *That sounds wonderful, Paula. But what about in my professional life? How do I live authentically and show up as myself when I go to work?*

Look, I get it. Some people (myself included) have lived a career of code-switching, not bringing our whole selves to our work environment, or simply choosing to wear a mask while working and then taking it off the moment we log off or leave our job.

Let me stop for a moment and define code-switching; it's when a person detaches themselves from aspects of their cultural or racial identity to assimilate to a dominant culture and comfort others in hopes of avoiding discrimination. Some of you may not relate to this, and if you don't, I am happy for you. But regardless, I want you to take notice of this because this is where the world of Diversity, Equity, and Inclusion (DEI) comes into play. We must create a culture and environment where everyone feels included and can bring their whole selves to their work environment. Our culture has made these words feel dirty, which is incredibly sad because DEI *is* leadership.

At one of my workshops for an organization, we talked at length about what "masking" and "not bringing our full selves" meant. This discussion generated immediate responses from some of the staff, who openly stated they didn't bring their full selves to work. Other staff members were surprised by the conversation and, more importantly, that their co-workers didn't feel comfortable bringing their whole selves to work. This is so important when we talk about living authentically because if you have to mask some part of yourself at work, it can lead to stress, anxiety, and frustration, which, let's be clear, *will* show up in your work.

As a Black woman, I have participated in and witnessed many discussions. Remember when I talked about the consequences of showing up authentically? I will never forget early in my career when I showed up as I was—direct, clear, and results-focused—and didn't get a promotion that I was qualified for. I contacted the hiring manager for feedback on why I didn't get the job. He, a white male, told me that I was too aggressive in my style. I was floored. Up to this point, I had received excellent reviews, promotions, and no concerns about my style. When I realized who had received the position, I told the manager I was stunned. I didn't get the role, but the person who received it was similar in style and even more "aggressive" than me. It was explained to me that the person who received the job had been applauded for being direct and getting results. I quickly realized what was happening: I had been deemed the "angry Black woman." This experience resulted in me leaving the company. Before I left, the hiring manager reached out because he didn't understand why I was leaving. I explained and moved on.

Now fast forward two years later. I returned after being recruited. This same manager asked to speak to me, and he apologized for what happened during the interview. He now understood he was wrong and that there was bias in play. Here's my thing: I appreciated the apology, but we don't realize that in situations like this, it impacts people's lives—from the staff affected by a person leaving and the ones who end up following the person leaving to the clients who lose out and many more. Our biases show up repeatedly, and we must be honest about them and continually check ourselves when they show up, even when we aren't called out on them. I could write a whole other book on this.

That being said, I didn't change my style, nor did I become less authentic; it simply taught me that I would not always get the results I wanted or deserved due to who I was and how I showed up. This awareness served me well in my later years as a leader. To this day, I am clear about who I am—and I am still growing!

Know What You Won't Tolerate

Let me be clear: living authentically doesn't mean tolerating everything. One of the most powerful signs of authenticity is knowing what you *won't* put up with. Too often, people confuse being authentic with being endlessly agreeable or "nice." But real authenticity is about alignment between your values, your voice, and your boundaries. What I mean is this:

- You can be kind and still draw a line.
- You can be respectful and still say, "Not in this space."
- You can be a team player and still know when it's time to walk away.

Authenticity isn't about pleasing others; it's about honoring yourself. And that starts by deciding what you will and will not tolerate, both personally and professionally. You don't have to accept everything to be authentic. You just have to stop accepting what doesn't honor *you.*

ACTION CHANGES THINGS

Reflect: How can I live authentically—for real?

1. What am I currently tolerating that's out of alignment with who I am?
2. Where am I shrinking, silencing, or shifting myself just to make others comfortable?
3. What needs to change—and am I willing to take the first step?

Quick Win: Pick one day and block 30–60 minutes on your calendar just for you. No guilt. No multitasking. Just you and whatever fills your cup—music, movement, a nap, journaling, silence—your call. Living authentically starts with knowing what brings you peace.

"Be intentional about how you show up because the world is waiting to meet the real you!" —Paula R Jenkins

NOTES

____

____

____

____

____

____

____

____

____

____

____

4

Being Financially Authentic

"Money won't create success; the freedom to make it will."
— commonly attributed to Nelson Mandela

Many years ago, my husband and I looked at our combined W2s, which reported hundreds of thousands of dollars in earnings, and said: "But where is all the money?" It made me pause and recognize that we had a problem, and I knew we weren't alone.

This is why I still, to this day, find that financial coaching is part of my gift to the world. Being financially authentic is hard. Period. I have spent years coaching and giving workshops on financial wellness to individuals, couples, organizations, youth, and young adults. I have seen a lot, but what I see most often is that people need to genuinely talk about where they are financially—and they don't like to do this. Why? Because of how society interprets financial authenticity. One of my first clients said, "Please don't judge me." In that moment, I realized people don't ask for help because they don't want to be judged. But I am here to tell you that many options for help are in the no-judgment zone. Which is why I needed to have a chapter dedicated to financial authenticity because I know so many people live inauthentic lives regarding their finances and are too ashamed to ask for help.

I could write a whole book on this—and honestly, I will! But for now, let's talk about what being financially authentic means and how we can get you there.

CHAPTER FOUR · BEING FINANCIALLY AUTHENTIC

"I Can't Save" — Or So She Thought

01 THE SITUATION
She was 55, married, and had no savings. None. She was also in debt, didn't budget, and — most importantly — couldn't see a way out.

02 THE CHALLENGE
The first thing she told me was something I hear all the time: "I don't have enough money to save." The real challenge wasn't her income. It was awareness, habits, and priorities.

03 WHAT WAS AT STAKE
This wasn't just about money. It was about her future, her ability to retire, her peace of mind, and her freedom. One thing was clear: she did not want to work forever.

04 THE TURNING POINT
We started with the basics: tracking her spending, building a real budget, and identifying where her money was actually going. Then came the hard part — being honest about what she was spending, what wasn't serving her, and what truly mattered.

05 THE AUTHENTIC SHIFT
We didn't do anything flashy. We got intentional. We uncovered money she didn't realize she had, cut expenses that didn't align with her lifestyle, prioritized what actually mattered — and made saving a non-negotiable habit.

06 THE RESULT
By the end of our work together, she had saved thousands. She had a system. She had clarity and confidence. And she understood something she hadn't before: saving isn't about how much you make — it's about what you choose to do with it.

Most people don't have a money problem. They have a clarity problem.

REFLECT

1. *Are you telling yourself you can't save... or choosing not to?*
2. *Do you actually know where your money is going?*
3. *What are you prioritizing that may not align with your future?*

ACT — THIS WEEK

Track your spending for 7 days. No judgment. Just awareness. Because you can't change what you refuse to look at.

REFLECT

1. *Are you spending in alignment with your lifestyle — or against it?*
2. *Do you actually know what your "wants" cost?*
3. *Are you planning your life... or reacting to it?*

ACT — THIS WEEK

Choose one lifestyle expense you love. Create a plan to fund it — before you spend it. Because the goal isn't restriction. It's freedom without regret.

Let's Ground This in Reality

If you think your money habits are just about numbers... they're not. There's real data behind why so many people feel stuck financially.

Financial Stress

Research shows:

According to the American Psychological Association, money is consistently one of the top sources of stress for Americans. Financial pressure impacts mental and emotional well-being, contributing to anxiety, relationship strain, and even long-term health issues.

Why it matters:
If your money is out of alignment, your life will feel it.

Emergency Savings Gap

Research shows:
Data from the Federal Reserve shows that many Americans would struggle to cover a $400 emergency expense without borrowing or selling something. That means a single unexpected event can disrupt financial stability.

Why it matters:
Without a cushion, every surprise becomes a crisis.

Living Paycheck to Paycheck

Research shows:
Recent reports from LendingClub show that a large percentage of Americans live paycheck to paycheck, with most of their income going directly to expenses and little left for savings or long-term planning.

Why it matters:
When all your money is already spent, your future doesn't get a vote.

So this isn't just about budgeting.
It's about control, clarity, and the life you're trying to build.

And if you've ever said, "I make enough—I just don't know where it goes…"

you're not alone.

What Is Financial Authenticity and Why Does It Matter?

Being financially authentic is an integral part of authenticity. Doing so can help you create a healthier relationship with money and cultivate financial health. It's about being honest and open with others in regard to your finances, income, debts, investments, and future goals. When we are financially authentic, it means we are taking ownership of our financial decisions and being honest with ourselves about our current situation. This can be challenging, but it's essential to creating financial success.

Being financially authentic also means that you can talk openly and honestly with those around you, whether they're friends, family, or colleagues. This helps to build trust and create a more secure financial future for everyone involved. This is an essential step because it allows you to manage your money honestly, leading to better decision-making and setting you up for long-term success.

Let's walk through three areas—savings, debt, and behavior—that I have seen decimate people's lives because they were unprepared.

Savings: Start Small, Stay Consistent

- Start with what you have—even if it's $5 per paycheck.
- Make saving a habit, not an afterthought.
- Pay yourself first. Always.

We've all heard the statistics: most Americans can't afford a $400 emergency. This is unsurprising. The reality is people are doing their best, and savings is usually one of those buckets that only gets filled occasionally. A lot of people were never taught about finances or how to save. And for those who were, you have been blessed with excellent knowledge.

As part of being financially authentic, the focus should be to pay yourself first every check. That means putting something aside—even if it's just $5. You have to make saving a part of your lifestyle. Once it's a habit, it won't feel so impossible anymore. The COVID pandemic taught us all a harsh lesson about being prepared for an emergency. So begin today and save something!

I have provided financial coaching to many clients over the years, but one sticks out the most, particularly around savings. This client was a married, fifty-five-year-old woman who didn't have any savings, was in debt, did not budget, and could not see a solution to their problem. One of the first things people will tell me is they don't have enough money to save, but in most cases, this is inaccurate. We must be intentional about saving and honest with ourselves about what we spend our money on. We worked together for nearly a year, working on her budget, uncovering money, removing expenses that were counterintuitive to her lifestyle, and getting clear on what was important to her.

By the time we finished our work together, she not only had thousands saved, but she was also clear about the importance of putting money aside with each check and about what her wants and needs meant for her lifestyle. She had to make decisions that impacted her future because she didn't want to work forever. You can save; the key is to make sure you are focused on what's truly important to you.

Debt: Face It, Don't Fear It

- Make a full list of every debt—yes, even the ones hiding in your email inbox.
- Pick one method: **snowball** (smallest first) or **avalanche** (highest interest first) then *stick to it*.
- Stop the bleeding—pause new debt while you tackle the old.

Debt has overtaken many people—credit cards, medical bills, car notes, personal loans, mortgages, student loans, timeshares, 401(k) loans, and more. Just thinking about personal debt can be debilitating.

The best way to tackle your debt is to first stop accumulating it and then work on paying one bill down at a time. There are multiple models to help pay down debt. Start somewhere. I know it can be overwhelming. I have had clients with $500,000 in personal debt and those with $10,000 in debt. Regardless of the amount, they needed help figuring out where to start. It can be paid down, and yes, it will take time, but if you are going to be financially authentic, you have to make sure you know where you're starting. So create that list—write down every debt you owe—and then begin creating a plan. You can do it!

I had a forty-year-old client who was single and loved to travel, but she was consistently going into debt due to her frequent trips. I knew I could help her solve this issue, as she made enough money but was not allocating funds correctly. We worked together for six months, and during this time, I helped her create a travel slush fund as part of her various bank accounts. We focused on putting a set amount of money in that fund from each paycheck. We also outlined what it takes for her to travel and feel comfortable, which is different for everyone. It's important to be authentic in this area of what you want and need when you travel. Once we outlined costs for transportation, lodging, food, excursions, and other items, we got an idea of how much she needed to save. Her first trip after going through this process was debt-free. It was a huge accomplishment. The lesson here was planning ahead and being authentic about her wants and needs. It really can be done!

Behavior: Your Mindset Is Your Money Mirror

- Be honest about your habits—your bank statement tells your real story.
- Identify where guilt, shame, or "keeping up" is driving your spending.

- Decide what truly matters and cut what doesn't—*without apology.*

Our behavior with money is fickle. We love to talk about what we can't afford and say things like, "I don't have enough to save or invest," yet we eat out all the time and spend money frivolously on things that don't provide a return on investment (ROI).

So what does this have to do with authenticity? Well, first and foremost, our financial situation so often impacts how we show up in the world, with our families, and at the workplace.

Upon first meeting one of my clients, she gladly announced, "I am that chick!" As a single, child-free woman, she claimed to be "that chick" who posts everything she buys—shoes, clothes, bags, you name it—on social media, but she is at home, broke! Immediately, I thought, *Well, that is self-awareness at its best.* This particular client made over $100K annually, but because of a severe spending problem, she had quite a bit of debt. She wanted to live a freer life, recognizing her faults but not knowing where to start.

This is a common situation, and understanding your cash flow (i.e., a budget—I know it's a dreaded word!) is the best place to start. Trust me, it works. Start by asking yourself: How much income is coming in? How much am I spending? You also have to give up some of the items you think are important, at least temporarily, like shopping for the sake of posting. It is hard initially, but it will be worth it when you see the difference in your situation.

When your money isn't right, it is so easy for it to show up negatively in your daily life. Money issues bring anxiety, frustration, pain, and embarrassment. Think about it this way: if you were happy with your current financial situation:

- How do you think this would show up in your relationships?
- How do you show up now?
- Are you living within your means?

- Above your means?
- Below your means?
- Are you staying at a job because you have to instead of because you want to?
- Are you living paycheck to paycheck?

I conducted a summer teen camp in 2023 that was focused on leadership and financial literacy. One of the statistics we discussed was that 78% of Americans live paycheck to paycheck. We talked about what it means to live this way, and they understood it, but they found it hard to believe how many people were doing so.

We must be honest with ourselves about where we are spending our money. There will always be factors outside of our control, but what is in our control is our behavior, and our behavior starts with our mindset about money. It goes back to how we were taught about money—that is, if we were taught anything. Once you identify your beliefs regarding money, you can unpack why you behave the way you do now and make the necessary changes.

The true key, however, is in your willingness to make the change. The question is not if you "can"—I've seen it time and time again with clients. I have spoken to hundreds of people over the years, and anxiety is natural. Let's walk through a few specific scenarios.

Real Life Stories

Single with Kids

One of the hardest things in life is raising children. It is even more complicated when you do it alone with one income. I have had multiple clients who have tried to give their children the world but recognize they are in over their heads. I have worked with clients in this situation who make $60k and others who make $170k. Regardless of income, the key is understand that we can't give our kids everything, and we do a disservice to them when we try to. We overextend ourselves to a point where we feel like we can't escape the situation.

Society makes us think we should have our children in every available activity. It becomes too much for the child and our bank account. Focus on the needs of your child first. Then, see what you can truly afford for wants and wait to add additional items until you can afford them. I know it's hard, but remember that your job is to raise your child as best you can—that also includes teaching them about financial wellness.

Married Without Kids

When married couples don't have children, there is usually a surplus of income, but it may not feel that way because people so often live above their means. How awesome would it be if you lived off one income and saved or invested the entire second income? This is sometimes hard for couples to understand, especially since they must align on goals and what they want to accomplish.

This scenario usually involves each person's mindset about money, which must be discussed and dealt with to get to a place where they can be honest and open about their financial situation. Take the time to meet regularly to talk about your finances and engage with each other on what you want to accomplish. You would be amazed at what a consistent conversation about your finances can do for you and your situation.

Married with Kids

Just like with single parents, married parents try hard to give their children as much as they can, but in doing so, they don't live financially authentic, and they certainly don't set a good example for their children. It can further complicate the situation if both parents are not on the same page financially. I have seen this over and over again. The key is to talk, plan, and consistently review your finances and goals. Things change. Our children change. Our environments and jobs change. It's crucial to establish a budget that works for your family and allows you to feel like you aren't just working for the sake of paying bills, but that you, as parents, are getting rewarded as well.

Married with Grown Children

Often, married couples spend eighteen plus years caring for their children rather than focusing on themselves, their marriage, or life after kids. I had a client who once sent me a long email asking for help as they didn't know where to start. They were married with two grown children who they financially supported. We worked together for a year and turned their situation around by focusing on mindset, creating and following a budget, and identifying needs vs. wants. We also worked on how they could or couldn't support their adult children. Sometimes, the reality is that a person will neglect their situation to help others. While this is noble, it can be catastrophic for a family, so think long and hard about what you can and can't do for your grown children.

Conclusion: Why Financial Authenticity Is Important

I wanted to share some of these stories to let you know that you are not alone. I know it's hard to raise your hand and say you need help, but I want you to be true to yourself and ask for help if you need it. It's out here.

Being financially authentic means being true to yourself, your money, and your financial management values. It means being honest about your financial situation, understanding your spending habits, and setting goals that align with your values and priorities. It also means clearly understanding your financial resources and limitations and making conscious choices. Doing so allows you to be more resilient in the face of unexpected economic challenges and make better financial decisions.

ACTION CHANGES THINGS

Reflect: Am I being my authentic self when it comes to finances?

1. Where am I not telling the full truth (to myself or others) about my money—income, debt, or spending?
2. What does "enough" look like for me right now?
3. What boundary would make my money life truer (e.g., a spending cap, a clear "no," an honest convo, or an automatic transfer)?

Quick Win: For one week, write down *every dollar* you spend—yes, even the gas station coffee. At the end of the week, highlight any "surprises" or patterns.

"Sometimes, people can't see hope. I do what I do so they can see a different way—and know they're not alone."

—Paula R Jenkins

NOTES

5

Communicating Authentically

"When you show up authentically, you create the space for others to do the same. Walk in your truth." —Unknown

Communication isn't just talking; it's how we connect, correct, and lead. Everything begins and ends with it. So, let's dig into what authentic communication actually looks like—because if you can't say it clearly, you can't lead clearly. (*Reminder: In a prior chapter, we defined communication as "the exchange of information using words, tone, facial expressions, and behavior." It's not just what we say, it's how we show up when we say it.*)

I remember once being at a bridal shower in the early 2000s. During the shower, we played a game where all attendees were asked to name one of the most important attributes of a successful marriage. At the time, I had been married for about three years or so. I remember saying, "Communication is key." Oh, did I start a firestorm! I remember one of the women in attendance saying, "Communication is overrated!" She was so emphatic about it! All I could do was say "hmph" and leave it alone.

My point here is that communication is NOT overrated. In fact, we do not value it enough. Living authentically in the context of communication means being honest and open about your thoughts and feelings. It involves speaking up when you feel uncomfortable or need to be heard and actively listening to those around you to better understand their perspectives.

CHAPTER FIVE · COMMUNICATING AUTHENTICALLY

"I Have Something to Say" — Finding Your Voice

01 THE SITUATION

I had a coaching client referred to me because they struggled with speaking up in meetings. On the surface, they were doing their job well. But behind the scenes, it was costing them.

02 THE CHALLENGE

They weren't being considered for promotions or new opportunities. The perception was that they didn't have the knowledge — but that wasn't true. They had the ideas, the insight, the recommendations. They just weren't saying anything. In meetings, especially with upper management, they sat quietly. Meanwhile, in their head? They were loud.

03 WHAT WAS AT STAKE

This wasn't just about communication. It was about visibility, credibility, career growth, and opportunity. The unintended message being broadcast in every silent meeting: "I don't have anything to contribute." In the workplace, that message can derail a career.

04 THE TURNING POINT

As we worked together, we started unpacking why. Their background mattered. Their gender mattered. Their cultural experiences mattered. They had learned over time that maybe they shouldn't speak up. Maybe it wasn't their place. Maybe it was safer to stay quiet — even in rooms they fully belonged in.

05 THE AUTHENTIC SHIFT

We worked on confidence, mindset, preparation, and small, intentional actions. Not jumping from silence to speeches — but from silence to one moment of contribution. Then another. Then another.

06 THE RESULT

Over time, everything changed. This same client — who once sat silently in meetings — now walks in with confidence. And when they have something to say? They say it. "I have something to say." And people listen.

Your silence is still communication — and it sends a message. Authentic communication is about being present, intentional, and willing to be heard.

REFLECT

1. *Where are you staying silent when you have something to say?*
2. *What are you afraid will happen if you speak up?*
3. *What message is your silence sending?*
4. *Do you believe you belong in the room?*

ACT — THIS WEEK

Commit to speaking up once in a meeting. Not five times. Not perfectly. Just once. Prepare one thought, one question, one perspective. And when the moment comes, say it:

"I have something to say."

Because your voice is not optional — it's necessary.

Let's Ground This in Reality

If you think communication is just about what you say… it's not. There's a reason your message doesn't always land the way you expect.

Emotional Intelligence & Communication

Research shows:
Daniel Goleman's work on emotional intelligence shows that effective communication isn't just about delivering a message—it's about managing yourself in the moment. Leaders who can regulate their emotions, read the room, and respond instead of react communicate more effectively and build stronger relationships.

Why it matters:
If you can't manage yourself, you can't manage the message.

Nonverbal Communication Impact

Research shows:
Psychologist Albert Mehrabian found that when verbal and nonverbal messages don't align, people tend to believe what they see and feel over what they hear. Body language, tone, and energy often carry more weight than words alone.

Why it matters:
You can say the right thing and still send the wrong message.

Transparency Builds Trust

Research shows:
Research from Edelman shows that employees are more likely to trust leaders who communicate openly and honestly—even during uncertainty. When leaders don't communicate clearly, people fill in the gaps, and that's where confusion and mistrust begin.

Why it matters:
Silence doesn't protect trust—it erodes it.

And if you've ever said, "That's not what I meant…"

this is why.

So communication isn't just about speaking.
It's about how people experience you when you do.

Adapting Without Disappearing

You don't need to change who you are to connect with others, but you do need to adjust how you show up based on the situation. That's not fake; it's *skillful.*

Think of it like this: I'm the same Paula whether I'm teaching college students or coaching executives, but how I *speak* to them shifts.

I'm still direct, but I adjust my tone, pace, and focus based on the relationship dynamic.

In other words, knowing your truth doesn't mean shouting it the same way to every person. It means showing up as yourself and being mindful of how others can best receive you. Because authentic communication isn't rigid; it's responsive. It means expressing your thoughts, feelings, and needs rather than hiding behind a façade or trying to please others. It also means being open to different perspectives and engaging in constructive dialogue and compromise. You can be respectful of others while still avoiding manipulation or deceit in your communication.

We come across different people in different situations in our lives. How I speak to my child vastly differs from how I talk to my spouse. How I speak to my co-worker differs from how I talk to my best friend. This does not mean that we change who we are when communicating; it just means that how we convey our message differs based on the relationship.

An important key here is knowing who you are. Once you understand how you communicate, you can start learning about those around you. When you know the answers to these questions, you can show up better with others when communicating:

- Are you a direct type of communicator?
- Are you a relaxed, social communicator?
- Are you data-driven and analytical when communicating?

These are just a few of the questions you should be asking yourself, and once you know who you are, you can help those around you by learning who they are next!

I am a strong proponent of assessments and understanding your communication style. I use them in my work with clients all the time. There are many out there, and they all can be used to help you understand your communication style. As I mentioned earlier, I focus on the DISC model. The DISC Assessment focuses on four communication styles:

- **Dominant:** "This person jumps straight to solutions. They'll say, 'What's the point?' or 'Let's get to the bottom line.'"
- **Influencing:** "They're talkative, full of stories, and usually smiling. They want to connect before they decide."
- **Steady:** "They're the ones who ask how your weekend was—and care. They dislike sudden changes and want everyone to get along."
- **Compliant:** "This person has a spreadsheet for everything. They ask lots of questions, need the details, and prefer accuracy over speed."

We're all a mix, but most of us usually lead with one or two styles. Knowing yours helps you show up more intentionally—and stop taking other people's styles personally. If you have never taken a communication assessment, I encourage you to do so; check out the QR code that comes with this book to get more information. Start with self-awareness of who you are.

I want to tell my story, which I often mention in my keynotes and workshops. If I were to say 180 over 140, what immediately comes to mind? Yes, most people will say blood pressure—very high blood pressure, to be exact. Well, you would be correct. This was my blood pressure in October 2017. I had gone to the doctor and knew it was high—I could feel it. My doctor immediately said if you don't change your environment, you are going to die. She was that direct and to the point. I appreciate her style to this day. At that moment, I realized something had to change.

So, how did I get there? Well, it was due to poor communication with my manager at work. As leaders, we are so focused on what we *think* our direct reports need that we fail to ask them directly. This was my situation. I had been assigned a new manager months earlier, and I was transparent in my first conversation about my communication style (being direct), my need to grow, and how I was looking and applying for other roles. My new manager stated he was also direct and would get me to like my job. Problem #1: Never tell a person what you will make them do when they tell you where they currently are. I digress. The following six months were tough.

As time passed, he removed me from meetings and emails, and my direct reports started asking why I wasn't on calls or email communications. I directly asked my manager why he was removing me, and his response was that since I was looking at other roles, I only needed to be part of some conversations. WOW. Talk about passive-aggressive behavior. Here's the thing: no matter where your employee is, if they are leading people and clients and don't have a new role, never remove them without conversing. Nonetheless, within three months of my 180/140, I left corporate America to become an entrepreneur and haven't looked back. There is much to learn here, but the key is how we communicate.

As leaders, you must communicate well in everything you do and understand how to speak to those around you. Do a self-assessment of how you communicate, and think about things like:

- Are you that leader who schedules meetings with your direct reports, and you don't show up? And you don't communicate? Why? Ouch.
- Are you that person who yells at your co-workers or staff and thinks this is the best way to get your point across? If so, STOP. You are not talking to children; you are talking to adults. So, show respect to those you work with and keep in mind that yelling is one of the most significant signs of disrespect.
- Are you that leader who says one thing to your staff, co-worker, or team and does something completely different without explaining the reasoning behind it? You lose credibility when you do this.

- Are you that person who doesn't understand the structure of a team, organization, or environment, so you make assumptions about someone's motives without pausing to understand? Take the time to learn before you state what should be done or why you don't think something should be done. Respect the process and those who are in the roles they are in.

Communicating authentically is important personally and professionally because it allows us to be honest, open, and genuine in our interactions with others. It encourages authenticity in all aspects of communication, from verbal conversations to written exchanges. Authentic communication helps create trust and understanding between individuals. It also allows us to express ourselves clearly and accurately, reducing feelings of miscommunication or misunderstanding.

Generations Communicate Differently

Every generation brings its own style:

- **Boomers** often prefer phone calls or face-to-face discussions.
- **Gen X** likes clear, concise emails and value autonomy.
- **Millennials** want efficient, tech-savvy communication, often via text or Slack.
- **Gen Z** prefers voice notes, DMs, and authentic, unfiltered conversation. They don't want corporate speak; they want real talk.

If you lead or collaborate across generations, don't assume your way is the only way. Flex your style, but don't fake your tone. That's authentic leadership in action.

Communication Method Can Make a Difference

Similarly to how different generations have unique communication styles, it's also common to shift your style across various methods of communication.

Face-to-Face

Face-to-face is the best way to communicate authentically because it allows us to be present in the moment while we're speaking. We can see the person's facial expressions, body language, and mannerisms, which all give us insight into their feelings or thoughts. Face-to-face communication also allows us to have a more meaningful dialogue. We can ask questions, provide clarity, and give honest opinions without worrying as much about potential miscommunication or misinterpretation.

Face-to-face communication is also the best way to show authenticity and build trust in relationships. It encourages us to be vulnerable and open about our feelings with less fear of judgment or rejection. Communicating face-to-face is the best way to ensure your authenticity is seen and heard, so don't be afraid to make yourself vulnerable.

Phone Calls

Communicating via phone can be a great way to stay connected and authentic when face-to-face interaction isn't possible. It allows us to hear the tone of voice and inflection in the person's words, which can help us better understand their feelings. Phone conversations also allow us to be vulnerable and honest without the added pressure of being face-to-face, which can be especially beneficial for those who are uncomfortable expressing themselves in person. We can still express our feelings, thoughts, and opinions but in a non-intimidating way.

Phone conversations can be a great way to stay connected and communicate authentically, so don't be afraid to pick up the phone and make a call.

Text Messages

Oh yes, we have to talk about this! Text messages can be a great way to communicate quickly and easily, but there are pros and cons to this form of communication. First, the pros: Texting allows us to send short messages that can still convey our authenticity. We can express ourselves now without worrying about filtering our words or being judged for what we say. It also allows us to avoid uncomfortable conversations or complex topics that can be hard to discuss face-to-face.

The downside of texting, however, is that it can be easy for our authenticity to get lost in translation. Messages can come across differently than intended without the added context of facial expressions, body language, or tone of voice. This can lead to feelings of miscommunication or misunderstanding.

In addition, it is sometimes less reliable than we think. Recently, I had two incidents where I received emails from people checking in on me because I had yet to respond to their text messages. I checked and asked for screenshots. Guess what? I never got them. Who knows how many other messages I may not have received? So the lesson here is to pick up the phone or try other communication methods; you never truly know if someone got it.

Texting can be a great way to communicate quickly and easily. Still, it is important to remember that authenticity can sometimes get lost in translation, so don't be afraid to pick up the phone or meet in person for more meaningful conversations.

Email

Emails can be a great way to communicate professionally and convey authenticity, but just like with texting, there are pros and cons to this form of communication. Emails allow us to express ourselves more fully than texts or phone calls. We have time to craft our thoughts into meaningful words that reflect our authenticity without the length limitations or a text or the timing restrictions of a phone call. Emails also allow us to avoid uncomfortable conversations or complex topics that can be hard to discuss face-to-face.

The downside of emails is that they can easily be misinterpreted and lead to feelings of miscommunication or misunderstanding. Messages can come across differently than intended without facial expressions, body language, and tone of voice. In addition, as I have learned the hard way, emails can be routed to your spam/junk folder or can be quarantined and go undelivered, so it's critical that multiple methods are used. Again, don't be afraid to pick up the phone for more meaningful conversations.

Vulnerability

Communicating vulnerably is an integral part of authenticity. Vulnerability allows us to open up, be honest, and express our true selves. When we communicate vulnerably, we are being authentic. We expose our weaknesses, doubts, and fears to build trust and connection with others. We are also showing our authenticity through our words and actions. Communicating vulnerably is not always easy, but it can be a compelling way to connect with others and show the world your true self.

Vulnerability is one of those things that most people are not comfortable with, but the power of it can change the world and those around you. During the pandemic, I had been more vulnerable than ever in my entire life. I am grateful for those moments. Why? Because I had many people reach out to say thank you for being human, thank you for being authentically me, thank you for sharing. There is power in being vulnerable.

It is so important that we take time to do self-reflection, as it makes us more self-aware of how we are showing up. Ask yourself:

- When was the last time I was vulnerable?
- How did I feel afterward?
- What was the impact on those around me?
- What do I want in life?
- What is my vision?
- Do those around me know this?

My vision is to help as many people as I can to become the best, most authentic leaders they can be. Do those around you know your vision? How are you communicating what is important to you? Communicating authentically allows you to live a far more fulfilling life because it's unsurprising to people why you do what you do, whatever that may be. Try to tell those around you what you want to accomplish. Now, I get it. Some people need more time to prepare for their vision. Some people won't understand it. Some people won't support you, whether that is family or friends. Hear me out though: leave them where they are; this is your vision. Get around people who will help you. Get around people so that when you communicate your vision and your dreams, they are there to cheer you on. You deserve it. Don't let *anyone* tell you otherwise.

ACTION CHANGES THINGS

REFLECT:

What conversations have you been avoiding?

1. Where did I edit myself today—and why?
2. How can I keep my message the same while adjusting my delivery for this person/situation?
3. What boundary or need do I need to communicate more clearly to someone?

Quick Win: Take some time to have a conversation you've been avoiding, then reflect on how the conversation went and what the outcome was.

"Do not stress over what you can't control.

Focus on your reaction." —Paula R Jenkins

NOTES

6

Social Media Authenticity

"Social media is not about the quantity of your posts; it's about the quality of your posts." — commonly attributed to Chris Brogan

In October 2020, I read an article called "Be Yourself: Authenticity on Social Media Leads to a Happier Life" that referenced a study from Columbia Business School which found that people who express themselves authentically on social media are happier and more satisfied with their lives (Columbia Business School, 2020). Go figure!

Remember, "I am that chick!"? This client told me she posts all the clothes she buys, where she goes, etc.—but she is at home, broke! I will always remember this because it truly speaks to what we, as a society, see but don't talk about. This woman admitted it openly and understood who she was—talk about self-awareness!

Here's the thing though: what you see on social media is not always accurate. We are made to believe that so many people are living happily and luxuriously. Social media is the biggest platform for these falsehoods. Those anniversary pictures of couples sharing they have been married 5, 10, 15, or 20 years? They might be fighting like cats and dogs, not sleeping in the same bed, and having severe marital strife. Yet, someone is looking at those pictures and thinking, "Woe is me because I don't have that." Nope, you don't want that! Those pictures of your friend going on a fabulous trip, showing you where they stayed, what they ate, and where they snorkeled? They might be charging the whole vacation to a credit card and late on bills without a dime in savings. Those pictures of their children scoring this play, going on this trip, or having all A's? That child might be disrespecting their parents at home, going through serious mental health issues, or experiencing a crisis that is too painful to talk about.

Let me be clear: I am not making light of any of the "realities," but what I am saying is let's be careful about how we perceive social media. Let's be more authentic about what we post, or at the very least, don't post any false narratives. In many cases, it does more damage than good.

In fact, research published in *Computers in Human Behavior* indicates that young adults who perceive themselves as authentic on social media report fewer mental health symptoms, such as stress and depression, over time (Bunker et al, 2024). Additionally, excessive social media use has been linked to increased risks of depression, anxiety, loneliness, and even suicidal thoughts, particularly among adolescents (The Annie E. Casey Foundation, 2024).

Ultimately, I'm not saying you need to immediately delete all of your social media accounts in order to live a happy and authentic life. But what I am saying is that what you see on social media isn't real. Don't compare yourselves to anyone because you don't know their story—and everyone has one. They just might not be sharing it.

"That's Not the Whole Story"

01 THE SITUATION

There was a time when I saw someone on social media who looked like they had it all together. The trips. The clothes. The celebrations. The life. And if I'm honest, for a moment, I thought: "Wow… they are really doing it."

02 THE CHALLENGE

The challenge with social media is this: it's easy to believe what you see. It's easy to compare, to question your own life, to feel like you're behind. Because when everything looks perfect, it's hard not to measure yourself against it.

03 THE REALIZATION

Then I found out the truth. Behind those posts was stress. Behind those pictures was debt. Behind that "perfect life" was pressure to keep up an image that wasn't real. I've had clients admit it plainly: "What I post is not my reality." And when you're comparing your real life to someone else's highlight reel — you will lose every time.

04 THE AUTHENTIC SHIFT

Now, when I'm on social media, I remind myself: this is a snapshot — not a full story. And when I post, I make a choice. To show up as me. Not perfect. Not polished. Just real. Because the goal is not to impress people. It's to connect with them.

05 THE RESULT

That shift changed how I engage online. Less comparison. More awareness. More intention. And more importantly — more alignment with who I actually am, not who I think people want to see.

06 THE TRUTH

If you're not careful, social media will have you comparing your real life to someone else's performance. Authenticity is not about visibility. It's about alignment.

We can make anything look good.But that doesn't make it real.

REFLECT

1. *Where have I compared myself unfairly online?*
2. *What kind of content makes me feel less than?*
3. *Am I posting to connect... or to impress?*

ACT — THIS WEEK

Unfollow, mute, or limit three accounts that make you feel out of alignment with who you are. Then do one of the following:

- Post something real.
- Or don't post at all — and connect with someone directly.

Because authenticity is not about visibility. It's about alignment.

Let's Ground This in Reality

If you think social media is "just entertainment"... it's not.
How you show up—and what you consume—has a real impact on your well-being.

Authenticity & Well-Being Online

Research shows:
Research from Columbia Business School found that people who present themselves more authentically on social media report higher levels of life satisfaction. Instead of curating a perfect image, expressing real thoughts, experiences, and identity contributes to a stronger sense of self and improved mental well-being.

Why it matters:
When you stop performing online, you start feeling better offline.

And if you've ever felt worse after scrolling than you did before...

this might be why.

So this isn't just about what you post.
It's about how social media is shaping how you see yourself.

Needing Acceptance vs. Showing Acceptance

I will be honest: I am not a fan of social media. Those who know me know I don't like it. I am on it because I have to be due to my business, but if I didn't, I would not!

So many people are so focused on the number of likes they get. Some part of us is craving that human connection and acceptance, and we turn to social media for validation. But at the same time, it amazes me how we have diminished the power of our words. A person can change their photo profile, and it gets hundreds of likes and comments. Yet, when they write a long, sincere post (authenticity!) or some other text, it barely hits three likes! I would love to see us get to the point where we engage with people again via a phone call—what a difference it would make.

That being said, let's try to use social media in an authentic way to take that human connection one step further—not just liking a post and going about your day. If you see someone posting and it moves you in a way, reach out to them. They may need you to reach out in order to live their authentic life. They may need you to reach out in order to leave their current toxic situation. They may need you to reach out in order to encourage them to get the help they need. There is such power in reaching out to someone after reading an impactful post. I've done it, and I've had it happen to me. Now, this doesn't mean that a person will be ready to receive your message at all times, but it shows that you saw it and wanted to share that you heard it.

Importance of Offline Connections

So, tell me about those 5,000 friends you have... I have been tickled over the years when I have received a friend request from someone, and when I accept it, it says they have reached their limit. Hmmm, so do you want me to be your "friend"? Do you even check your page before sending it out?

We have gotten to this space where it is expected that we know what's going on with everyone because it's posted on social media. Well, I don't, and let me take a moment to thank all of my people who reach out to me when an important update about them or someone we know in common is posted, and they *know* I won't see it.

All this to say: check in with people. Those social media algorithms are daunting, and we don't see most of what is posted. I want to encourage you to foster real-life relationships and engage in offline activities. This can help mitigate the negative effects of excessive social media use. We love people who follow us and like our posts, but relationships come from building trust and authenticity. Make sure you don't just engage on social media. Reach out via text, phone, email, or even a letter—*GASP!* Do you know how excited I get when I receive a letter? Take a moment this week and write to someone! It will make their day.

Here is the last thing I will say on social media: put it into perspective and don't let it drive how you feel about yourself. Please know we can write or post anything we want, but it does not dictate the truth. And if you are posting, make sure to post authentically; you might make someone's day.

ACTION CHANGES THINGS

REFLECT:

How can you post with purpose and connect with intention?

1. Am I posting what's *true*, or what's expected?
2. What emotions do I feel when I scroll through social media?
3. What would it look like to share something that reflects who I am today?

Quick Win: Pick someone whose post you've recently "liked" or commented on. Instead of double-tapping their post, reach out and send them a text, call them, write a short email or (gasp!) a handwritten note.

"Your truth can be someone else's gift in their current situation." —Paula R Jenkins

NOTES

7

Praying with Authenticity

FAITHFULLY AUTHENTIC: PRAYING LIKE YOU MEAN IT

"Use me, God. Show me how to take who I am, who I want to be, and what I can do, and use it for a purpose greater than myself." — commonly attributed to Rev. Dr. Martin Luther King Jr.

There is a song that truly got me through the pandemic. There were a few, but one speaks to this chapter. It is called "Won't he do it" by Koryn Hawthorne. I played it daily for nearly twelve months. What I got from the song was inspiration that nobody's perfect, that I can choose to come and get my breakthrough, and then I will be able to look back and be so amazed at what God has done. I am an unapologetic believer in God, and my faith is truly important to me.

Given my faith, it was vital to talk about praying authentically when living and leading authentically. How could I not?

CHAPTER SEVEN · PRAYING WITH AUTHENTICITY

"We Showed Up Anyway."

01 — THE SITUATION

During the pandemic, five of us started a weekly prayer call. At first, it was just something to help us get through a hard time. A way to stay connected. A way to stay grounded.

02 — THE CHALLENGE

What started as survival became consistency. Week after week, we showed up. Not perfect. Not always strong. Not always with the right words. Just showing up. And let's be honest — there are moments in life when showing up is the hardest thing to do.

03 — THE REALIZATION

And then life happened. We lost one of our dear friends in the group. And even in that pain, we kept showing up. That's when it hit me. Prayer is not about saying the right thing. It's not about having it all together. It's about being honest. Some days we prayed in strength. Some days, in tears. Some days, we didn't have words at all. But we showed up.

04 — THE AUTHENTIC SHIFT

We stopped trying to "get it right." We let go of sounding perfect, having the right words, and feeling like we had to show up strong every time. And instead, we showed up as we were. Honest. Present. Real.

05 — THE RESULT

That consistency — that authenticity — deepened not only our faith, but our connection to each other. And even after everything we've been through, we still meet weekly to this day.

06 — THE TRUTH

Prayer is not about perfection. It is about presence. Showing up as you are — in whatever state you're in — is enough.

Prayer is not about perfection. It is about presence.

REFLECT

1. *Am I honest in my prayers?*
2. *Do I only pray when I need something?*
3. *What does consistency in prayer look like for me?*

ACT — THIS WEEK

Set aside one intentional prayer moment this week. No script. No performance. Just honesty.

Because showing up as you are… is enough.

Let's Ground This in Reality

If you think prayer is only spiritual… it's not.
There's a real impact on your mind, your body, and how you process life.

Prayer & Stress Reduction

Research shows:
Research from Harvard Medical School shows that when you slow down to pray, reflect, or be still, your body responds. Your mind begins to settle, and your nervous system shifts out of stress mode and into a calmer state.

Why it matters:
When you create space to be still, you give yourself space to breathe.

Spirituality & Coping

Research shows:
According to the American Psychological Association, during difficult moments, people often turn to prayer as a way to cope. It helps

process pain, create meaning, and navigate situations that don't always make sense.

Why it matters:
When life feels overwhelming, prayer gives you something to hold on to.

Gratitude & Prayer Connection

Research shows:
Dr. Robert Emmons' research on gratitude shows that regularly practicing gratitude—often through prayer—can significantly increase overall happiness and well-being.

Why it matters:
What you consistently acknowledge, you begin to experience more deeply.

And sometimes, just showing up—even without the right words—is enough.

So prayer isn't about having the right words.
It's about creating space to be honest, present, and grounded.

Faithfully Authentic
Being faithfully authentic is challenging in some cases. It means staying true to who you are and what you believe in, even when it's complicated. It's about having the courage to express your thoughts and feelings without fear of judgment or criticism. Authenticity is a commitment to being honest with yourself and others in all aspects of life, even if it takes you out of your comfort zone. Being authentic means showing up as your true, genuine self daily and taking ownership of your life, decisions, and emotions. It also means speaking up when something isn't right and standing up for your beliefs. Authen-

ticity is a journey that can lead to greater self-awareness and personal growth.

Likewise, being faithfully authentic in prayer means showing up with honesty and intention. Instead of reciting routine words or trying to fit a mold, it's about being real—naming your thoughts, feelings, fears, and hopes exactly as they are. It's choosing presence over performance.

Authentic prayer can take many forms: traditional prayer, silent meditation, journaling, or even a deep breath whispered with hope. The method doesn't matter as much as the meaning behind it. The key is being open, not just to asking but to listening, receiving, and giving thanks. That's where the connection grows deeper. That's where clarity and self-awareness often begin.

One of the best things about the pandemic was my weekly prayer call with four friends. We started the first week of the pandemic to give us some encouragement and support, and to pray at the end of each call. We are still at it five years later and closer than ever. We suffered a loss as our dear friend passed away in 2023. Yet, we still meet. It truly gives us something to look forward to every week. We are faithfully authentic every time we meet and have provided support through all of life's challenges. I love you, ladies!

Enemies

Let me say it plainly: when you lead with authenticity, not everyone is going to cheer you on. Some people just won't like you. They may misunderstand you, disagree with your approach, or quietly root for your failure. That's real. And it's *not* your problem.

I've seen it—and I've felt it. Especially in the online world, where people hide behind keyboards and say things they'd never have the nerve to say face-to-face. Social media has made it easy for people to be loud and nasty without accountability. This is one of the reasons I avoided YouTube for so long. I didn't want to deal with internet trolls who confuse cruelty for critique.

But I had a friend check me. He said, "I don't know you that well yet, but you don't strike me as someone who gives a #%&! about what people think." And he was right. Personally? I don't. Professionally? That took some work. Because your brand *does* matter. But so does your peace. And that's where prayer comes in.

If you're going to live and lead authentically, you'll need a practice—whether it's prayer, meditation, reflection, or therapy—that helps you stay grounded when the noise gets loud. Here's what I've learned about handling enemies while staying true to yourself:

- **Don't take the bait.** Not every attack deserves a response. Silence can be powerful.
- **Stay anchored in your values.** When you know who you are, you won't waste energy defending yourself to people who've already made up their minds.
- **Surround yourself with truth-tellers.** You need people in your life who don't just cheer you on, but who also remind you of who you are when the world tries to twist it.

And when all else fails, remember: there are people out there who didn't like Mother Teresa. Think about that. Stay focused. Stay faithful. Stay you.

Trust

Praying will feel more authentic if you learn to trust that everything will work out as it should. Trusting in prayer when living an authentic life means having faith in a higher power to guide and support you in your journey toward authenticity. It's about understanding that certain things are beyond our control and surrendering them to a higher power. This can help reduce anxiety and uncertainty and allow you to focus on being true to yourself.

Incorporating prayer into your authentic life journey also provides a valuable source of support and guidance. It can provide comfort and offer a sense of perspective when faced with difficult decisions. It can also give a sense of peace and inner strength in moments of self-doubt and insecurity. Trusting in prayer can also help you develop a greater sense of gratitude and appreciation for the present moment and what you have in your life. It can remind you that you are not alone in your journey and that a higher power is always with you, supporting and guiding you towards your goals and ideals.

I know it can be hard to trust in your prayer sometimes. This is where you truly must draw on your faith—and it's okay even to wonder if what is being done is what is supposed to happen. Life has ebbs and flows that we sometimes don't understand. But trust in your higher power, and you will live a more fulfilling life.

Trusting in prayer with authenticity also brings a sense of victory in self-discovery and personal growth. When we are true to ourselves in worship, we can connect with a higher power on a deeper level and receive guidance specific to our individual needs and circumstances. This can lead to a greater sense of inner peace and understanding of our purpose in life.

Additionally, when we trust in authentic prayer, we can let go of the need to control everything in our lives and instead trust a higher power to guide us. This can lead to a sense of liberation and freedom, as we no longer feel the world's weight on our shoulders. It also allows us to focus on living in the present rather than worrying about the future or dwelling on the past. Trusting in prayer with authenticity will enable us to cultivate a sense of gratitude and contentment, leading to a more fulfilling and joyful life. In this way, the victory that comes with trusting in prayer with authenticity is the ability to live a life that is true to ourselves and in alignment with our values and beliefs.

Once you trust, the victory does come, but it may not be as you thought. To all my prayer warriors: keep it up. The victories will continue to pile up because of your diligence and belief in whatever higher power you choose. Just know that praying with authenticity is where it begins.

ACTION CHANGES THINGS

REFLECT:

Are you praying with authenticity?

1. If I dropped the "right words," what would I honestly say in my prayers?
2. What am I willing to surrender that I can't control?
3. How will I listen after I pray (silence, scripture, walk, breath-work)—when and where?

Quick Win: Do a 5-minute "real prayer" using this four-line template: *Here's what's true... Here's what I need... Here's what I'm releasing... Here's one faithful step I'll take today...*

"My prayer is to show up authentically while living and

leading daily." —Paula R Jenkins

NOTES

8

Minding Your Authenticity

AUTHENTICITY STARTS WITH THE MIND

"Honesty and transparency make you vulnerable. Be honest and transparent anyway." — commonly attributed to Mother Teresa

We have all heard a lot about mental health and the importance of taking care of ourselves. One of the things that impacted me personally during the height of the COVID-19 pandemic was the sheer volume of people—both children and adults—whose mental health was attacked. The pain, solitude, and angst that were pervasive for months indeed took a toll on a lot of people. Amidst this, a truth was told: we weren't okay at all. And something good came out of this realization: we finally started talking about mental health—like *seriously* talking about it. Even in the midst of it, so many of us were still lonely, suffering in silence, and trying to manage getting an appointment with a therapist.

So, I must talk about how to mind your authenticity; our lives depend on it.

CHAPTER EIGHT · MINDING YOUR AUTHENTICITY

"I'm Fine... But I'm Not"

01 — THE SITUATION

I've worked with people who looked like they had everything together. Great job. Strong presence. High performance. And then you sit down with them... and the truth comes out: "I'm not okay."

02 — THE CHALLENGE

Not burned out enough to stop. Not broken enough to ask for help. Just stuck in between. Functioning — but not fulfilled. Showing up — but not present. And that's the dangerous place. Because when you stay there too long, it starts to affect your energy, your relationships, your leadership, and your health.

03 — THE REALIZATION

We've been taught to push through — the stress, the pressure, the expectations. But pushing through without processing? That's not strength. That's survival. And survival is not the same as living.

04 — THE AUTHENTIC SHIFT

At some point, something has to change. You have to stop pretending you're okay when you're not. You have to acknowledge what's actually going on — not for everyone else, but for you. That might look like saying it out loud, slowing down, asking for help, or simply admitting the truth to yourself.

05 — THE RESULT

When you allow yourself to be honest about where you are, you create space to actually move forward. Not from pressure. Not from performance. But from awareness. And that's where real change begins.

06 — THE TRUTH

You can look strong and still be struggling. Ignoring it doesn't make it go away — it just delays the impact. Awareness without action keeps you stuck.

> **You can look strong and still be struggling. Ignoring it doesn't make it go away — it just delays the impact.**

REFLECT

1. *Where am I saying "I'm fine" when I'm not?*
2. *What support do I need that I haven't asked for?*
3. *What is one area of my life being affected by what I haven't processed?*

ACT — THIS WEEK

Write down one way your mental health has been impacted lately. Then take one action:

- Book therapy.
- Talk to someone safe.
- Go for a walk, rest, or ask for help.

One step. Because awareness without action... keeps you stuck.

Let's Ground This in Reality

If you feel off... but can't quite explain why—there's a reason for that. And it's not random.

Authenticity & Mental Well-Being

Research shows:
Psychologist Carl Rogers introduced the idea that true psychological health comes from something called congruence—the alignment between who you are internally and how you show up externally. When there's a gap between the two, people often experience anxiety, stress, and a sense of disconnection.

Why it matters:
When who you are doesn't match how you're showing up, it will catch up to you.

And if you've been pushing through instead of processing…

this might be why you feel stuck.

So this isn't just about "being okay."
It's about being honest about where you are.

Mental Health—Let's Talk About It

It's okay—you aren't good! I'm not good! Our kids could be better. And nobody wants to talk about it. But we *must*.

Research shows that people who live more authentically are prone to greater psychological well-being. We know that greater mental health generally leads to greater physical health. If you aren't living as your authentic self, the stress that comes with inauthenticity impacts your body and mind.

Talking about mental health is essential because it helps to destigmatize the issue and encourages people to seek help when needed. Mental health affects everyone, but we all have different experiences, levels of resilience, and coping methods. By discussing mental health openly and honestly, people will start to understand that there is nothing wrong with or shameful about seeking support for their mental health. It can be challenging to talk about, but it is a vital step in helping people get the support they need. It encourages people to be open and honest about their experiences and to seek help without fear or shame. By talking openly and honestly about mental health, we can start to create a more supportive and understanding environment for those who are struggling.

Therapy: It's Time to Normalize It

Stop saying you're "fine" when you're not. Normalize therapy. It's not weakness; it's wisdom. A therapist helps you talk without being judged, held, or fixed. Just heard. You deserve that. Don't stop after one bad fit—shop around like it's your next favorite pair of jeans. When you do find the right one, it changes everything.

Getting a therapist is an important step in minding your authenticity. Working with a professional can help you explore what authenticity means to you and how you can best express it in both your personal life and through your leadership. A therapeutic relationship can be a safe space for self-discovery, reflection, and growth, helping you to understand yourself better and how you can show up as your true self.

Minding authenticity is not easy, but it is worth it; therapy can be an invaluable tool to support authenticity. A safe, supportive therapeutic relationship can provide the space for authenticity to thrive, helping you become the best version of yourself. So, if authenticity is something that you strive for, consider investing in a therapeutic relationship to help you realize your potential and to normalize it. Take the time to be true to yourself, and remember that authenticity is more important than perfection. Live your life and lead authentically. This will help create meaningful relationships with those around you. It is essential to remember that authenticity is more important than perfection, and investing in a therapeutic relationship can help you become the best version of yourself.

Self-Care Is a Leadership Skill

Self-care isn't selfish; it's how you lead from overflow instead of burnout. Whether it's walking, journaling, silence, or a hotel stay away from it all—take it. Schedule joy. If your tank is empty, you can't pour into anyone else. Your wellness is your witness.

I am a believer in it. I own it, and I take it. Find your routine—whatever it is. For me, it's walking outside for at least an hour daily. I have come to appreciate nature so much. It could also be yoga, running, boxing, gardening, volunteering, but whatever it is, make sure you take the time to ensure you are good. One of the things I did for about six months was take two days and work in a hotel. This allowed me a break, a different environment, and peace of mind. On top of that, I got the opportunity to walk along the beautiful lakefront of Chicago.

Self-care can take many forms—from getting enough sleep to taking time out to practice meditation or mindfulness. Whatever form it takes, self-care should be an integral part of your life to stay balanced and address any challenges that come your way.

In short, self-care is essential to authenticity because it provides the foundation for it to flourish. Investing in your self-care can make a world of difference, and it is worth the effort to do so. Take time for yourself to prioritize your well-being, and authenticity will follow!

Imposter Syndrome

Imposter syndrome is the feeling of not being worthy or good enough despite evidence of success. It can lead to feelings of inadequacy, insecurity, and self-doubt. People experiencing impostor syndrome are often paralyzed by the fear that they will be exposed as a "fraud" and that their accomplishments are undeserved or luck-based. Despite their successes, they may feel like an impostor and as though their success is not genuine. It's important to remember that most people experience impostor syndrome at some point; it doesn't make you unworthy or invalidate your achievements.

The most challenging part of imposter syndrome is facing your inner critic. This little voice inside you will whisper, "You don't belong here." I've heard that voice. With 30+ years of experience, I still hear it sometimes. But here's what I know: that voice is a liar. You belong. Your story matters. You earned your seat. Your authenticity is your authority. Say it with me: *"I'm not an impostor. I'm impactful."*

Imposter syndrome can make it difficult to be authentic, as it can be hard to separate the voice in our head from what is true. But we must challenge our negative thoughts and focus on self-acceptance to overcome impostor syndrome and mind authenticity. We must recognize that everyone makes mistakes and nobody is perfect; there will always be areas where we grow and learn. We must also be mindful of our strengths and focus on our achievements rather than dwelling on our weaknesses. In addition, it can help to practice self-compassion; don't be too hard on yourself, and remind yourself that authenticity is power.

If you're interested in learning more about imposter syndrome, there is a great article on the history of impostor syndrome by *Psychology Today* (Azab, 2023). You can find it in the resources section of this book.

Regardless of whether or not you struggle with imposter syndrome, it can help to connect with others and seek support from those who will encourage authenticity. Authenticity is power, so use it for good! Embrace it in all aspects of your life and watch its impact, not just for you but for those around you. Living and leading as your true self may seem daunting, but with practice and intentionality, you can make authenticity a part of your daily practice. Live and lead authentically, make a difference, and show the world that being who you are is worth it. Being yourself is power—so don't let imposter syndrome hold you back. Now go out and be unapologetically YOU. You are powerful.

ACTION CHANGES THINGS

REFLECT:

How are you currently prioritizing (or not prioritizing) your mental health?

1. Where am I saying "I'm fine" when I'm not? Name the real feeling.
2. What story about me isn't serving me—and what's a truer story I can live instead?
3. What support (therapy, rest, an honest convo) would make my mind feel more authentic?

Quick Win: Choose one non-negotiable self-care activity and schedule it.

"My self-care is my gift to those around me.

My self-care is not a luxury. It's how I lead." —Paula R Jenkins

NOTES

Emotionally Intelligent Authenticity

"Emotional intelligence is your ability to recognize and understand emotions in yourself and others, and your ability to use this awareness to manage your behavior and relationships." —Travis Bradberry

Let's be real: emotional intelligence isn't just for C-suite execs or therapists. It's for every one of us trying to live and lead in this messy, beautiful, unpredictable world. If you want to be an emotionally authentic leader (or human), you've got to stop avoiding how you feel and start using it to lead better. That's what this chapter is all about.

Before we dive deeper, let's get honest with ourselves. Emotional intelligence, or EI, is about recognizing, understanding, and managing emotions—both our own and others'. In this chapter, we'll use this four-part framework adapted from *Emotional Intelligence 2.0* by Travis Bradberry and Jean Greaves:

- **Self-Recognition**: Awareness of your own emotions and how they affect your behavior.
- **Self-Management**: Your ability to manage and regulate emotional responses effectively.

- **Social Recognition**: The capacity to recognize and understand emotions in others (hello, empathy!).
- **Social Management**: The ability to manage relationships and respond appropriately in social settings.

Now, before you read further, pause and reflect. Where are you *really* right now? On a scale of 1 to 5, with 1 meaning "I need serious growth here" and 5 meaning "I'm showing up strong," rank yourself in each of the four areas below.

- Self-Recognition: ____
- Self-Management: ____
- Social Recognition: ____
- Social Management: ____

Sometimes, we need a starting point to identify where we are coming from. I do this exercise in my workshops to level set because often, we need to first understand what EI truly is, especially when it comes to us individually, let alone when leading a team.

Emotional intelligence is often talked about when discussing leadership. It is an area that, while "talked" about, is so often overlooked. It is crucial to understand how it can impact you, your team, and those around you. Emotional intelligence is "the capacity to be aware of, control, and express one's emotions, and to handle interpersonal relationships judiciously and empathetically."

Korn Ferry Institute published a paper called "Emotional Intelligence—Why Now?" addressing "The Emotional Intelligence Gap." According to their research, only 22% of 155,000 leaders have real strengths in EI—where people see them as often or consistently showing at least 9 of 12 EI competencies. The remaining 88% of leaders show moderate strength or less (Korn Ferry Institute, 2021). There's a huge gap between the crying need for emotionally intelligent leadership and leaders' ability to deliver on that requirement. This is a concern, and we must address it.

CHAPTER NINE · EMOTIONALLY INTELLIGENT AUTHENTICITY
"Fix Your Face."

01 — THE SITUATION
I once had a friend tell me: "Congratulations on your promotion — but I'm going to need you to fix your face." Now listen… I laughed. But I also paused.

02 — THE CHALLENGE
In my mind, I thought I knew exactly how I was showing up. I was focused. I was driven. I was getting results. But what I didn't realize? My face was telling a whole different story. And if I'm honest, it probably wasn't saying anything positive.

03 — THE REALIZATION
That moment made me stop and think: how often do we believe we're showing up one way — while people are experiencing us completely differently? That's the gap. The gap between intention and impact. And that's where emotional intelligence lives. Because emotional intelligence is not just about how you feel. It's about how people experience you.

04 — THE AUTHENTIC SHIFT
I had to be honest with myself. Being results-driven wasn't enough. Being focused wasn't enough. If my presence was creating confusion or discomfort, then I had work to do. So I started paying attention to my expressions, my tone, and my energy — not to become someone else, but to make sure how I showed up aligned with who I actually am.

05 — THE RESULT
That awareness changed everything. Not overnight — but over time. I became more intentional. More aware. More aligned. And I understood that leadership is not just about what you do. It's about how people experience you while you're doing it.

06 — THE TRUTH
You don't get to define your impact — other people experience it. Emotional intelligence is the bridge between who you are and how you're received. Awareness is the first step, but adjustment is where growth happens.

> **You don't get to define your impact — other people experience it. Emotional intelligence is the bridge between the two.**

REFLECT

1. *How do people experience me when I'm stressed?*
2. *What do my face, tone, and energy communicate?*
3. *Have I asked anyone for honest feedback lately?*

ACT — THIS WEEK

Ask one trusted person:

"How do I show up when I'm under pressure?"

And when they answer — listen. Not to respond. Not to defend. Just to understand.

Because awareness is the first step — but adjustment is where growth happens.

Let's Ground This in Reality

If you've ever felt like you don't belong—even when everything says you do—you're not alone.
And it's not just in your head.

Imposter Syndrome

Research shows:
Psychologists Pauline Clance and Suzanne Imes first identified what we now call imposter syndrome—where high-achieving individuals struggle with persistent self-doubt and fear being exposed as a fraud. Even with clear evidence of their success, they often attribute it to luck rather than their own ability.

Why it matters:
When you don't believe you belong, you won't show up like you do.

And if you've ever thought, "They're going to find me out…"

that's exactly what this is.

So this isn't just about confidence.
It's about what you believe about yourself—and how that shows up in everything you do.

Let's talk about authentically being yourself in emotional intelligence, starting with self-recognition.

Self-Recognition: Who Are You, Really?

Can you name how you're feeling right now, without using "fine," "busy," or "tired"? If not, we've got some work to do.

Self-recognition is your ability to notice what's happening inside you. It's not just "Am I mad?" but "Why am I mad, and where did that come from?" You can recognize when you're triggered, when you're operating out of fear, and when your confidence is slipping.

I once had a coaching client who didn't realize they were reacting to their team from a place of burnout. They thought they were "just holding folks accountable." But guess what? They were exhausted and irritated, and it showed. Until they recognized their emotional state, their team couldn't trust them.

If you don't know how you feel, it's going to leak out in ways that hurt your communication, your leadership, and your authenticity.

Self-Management: Pause. Breathe. Think. React.

This is my mantra. I live it. I teach it.

Self-management is about what you do once you *do* recognize what you're feeling. Are you reacting out of instinct, or responding with intention?

Let me walk you through what I use when my attitude tries to come through:

- I **pause.** When a situation looks like it is getting out of control or if someone says something that is so out of pocket that you want to strike out, you must pause. So that's where I start now: I show up best by first pausing.
- I **breathe.** Take several deep breaths and try to quiet your mind as you do. It helps.
- I **think.** Here is the hard part. Why? We react automatically because who has time to think in a situation? But it's critical to take time to think about what you are going to do next and the impact of that action.
- And *then* I **react.** Once you have had a moment to think, it's now time to react. If the process has genuinely worked, your reaction will be far different from what it would have been had you not done the first three items. When you react now, it will be apparent that by pausing, breathing, and thinking first, you can show up how you want to—with a much clearer head.

One of the things I have had to work on in my walk of being authentically me is my patience and attitude. Yup, I could be better! In the past few years, as much as I have loved my authenticity, I have recognized that sometimes I must pause before I react. I learned this in various leadership roles. My initial reaction was to cuss someone out, but instead, I started to use my mantra: Pause. Breathe. Think. React.

This has saved relationships and opportunities, and most importantly, it has saved me from acting outside my character. I'm still a work in progress, but this mantra helps me lead and live without losing my integrity.

Social Recognition: See People. Really See Them.

Social recognition is where empathy lives.

When you walk into a room, do you notice what's *not* being said? Can you tell who's checked out or who needs to be heard? Social recognition is your ability to read the room. It's noticing tone, energy, body language, and emotional shifts—and not ignoring them.

I'll be honest, sometimes being emotionally tuned in means you carry more. But it also means you lead better, parent better, and love better. Because you're *aware*.

Social recognition means:

- You notice when someone is off.
- You ask the follow-up question.
- You stay present instead of brushing things off.

This isn't just emotional labor; it's emotional leadership.

Social Management: Lead With EQ, Not Just IQ

You can be brilliant, but if you can't collaborate, communicate, or coach, your leadership is limited.

Social management is how you manage relationships, resolve conflict, coach others, and drive culture.

Ask yourself:

- How do I handle hard conversations?
- Can I give feedback without making people defensive?
- Do I know when to shut up and let someone else shine?

Let me be clear: this is the EI sweet spot for leaders. Because it's where your influence either grows or dies.

ACTION CHANGES THINGS

Reflect:

Are you leading with emotional intelligence?

Remember that reflection we did at the start of the chapter? It's time to revisit it.

Rate yourself again on a scale of 1–5 (1 = I need work, 5 = I'm strong here):

- Self-Recognition: _______
- Self-Management: _______
- Social Recognition: _______
- Social Management: _______

Compare your before and after. What shifted?

Quick Win: Have one courageous conversation. Use your EQ to lead with intention. Don't ghost the hard stuff—show up in it. That's authenticity in action.

"Be you. Do you. Know you. Grow you." —Paula R Jenkins

NOTES

10

Intentionally Authentic

"Authenticity is more than speaking. Authenticity is also about doing. Every decision we make says something about who we are." — commonly attributed to Simon Sinek

The time has come to focus on the relationships in your life—and check how you're showing up in them. Not who people think you are. Who are you actually?

Being intentionally authentic means you don't live by accident. You're choosing, on purpose, to live out your values and stand in your truth. Yes, it can be uncomfortable. Yes, it can be lonely. But it's also freeing.

Let me be clear: being "authentically you" does *not* give you the right to be a jerk. It doesn't give you a pass to disregard others and say, "Well, that's just who I am!" No. This is about accountability *and* alignment. I don't apologize for being Paula. I know that might excite some people and annoy others. I'm not performing for either group. I'm here to show up fully for myself, and that has made all the difference.

Let's talk about a few different scenarios and how we can ensure we are being intentional in our authenticity.

CHAPTER TEN · INTENTIONALLY AUTHENTIC

"This Is Me."

01 THE SITUATION

There came a point in my life where I had to make a decision. Was I going to keep adjusting myself to fit what people expected? Or was I going to show up as who I really am?

02 THE CHALLENGE

Because let's be honest — that decision is not easy. Showing up as yourself means letting go of the polished version, the filtered version, and the version that makes everyone comfortable. And stepping into you. Fully.

03 THE REALIZATION

And here's what I had to come to terms with: when you decide to be fully yourself, some people will love it, some will question it, and some will walk away. That's the part we don't always want to accept. But it's real.

04 THE AUTHENTIC SHIFT

I had to decide: I am not here to be everything to everyone. I am here to be true to myself. Not sometimes. Not when it's convenient. But consistently.

05 THE RESULT

And once I made that decision, everything changed. Not because life got easier — but because I got clearer. Clear on who I am. Clear on how I show up. Clear on what I will — and won't — accept.

06 THE TRUTH

Intentional authenticity is a choice. You either decide to show up as yourself — or you keep performing for everyone else. At some point, you have to decide: this is me.

> **Intentional authenticity is a choice. You either decide to show up as yourself — or you keep performing for everyone else.**

REFLECT

1. *Where am I still editing myself for acceptance?*
2. *What would it look like to fully show up as me?*
3. *What am I afraid might happen if I do?*

ACT — THIS WEEK

Choose one area this week — family, friendship, work, or identity — and show up more honestly there.

- One conversation.
- One boundary.
- One truth.

"This is me."

Because at some point, you have to decide — and mean it.

How Do You Show Up?

As discussed in an earlier chapter, authenticity is essential for meaningful relationships. It builds trust. It creates space for honesty, real communication, and meaningful connection. When you show up as yourself with all your flaws, gifts, boundaries, and quirks, you permit others to do the same.

By being genuine with others, you show them you value authenticity and openness in your relationship. This helps to foster trust and understanding, which are necessary for solid relationships. Additionally, authenticity encourages growth both personally and collectively. Expressing yourself honestly creates an environment of safety where each person can be comfortable being their true selves. Authenticity allows for vulnerability and the possibility of mistakes, which are necessary for personal growth and developing a deep connection with the other person. Being authentic in relationships is not always easy, but it is worth it as it encourages understanding and builds more vital unions that will last.

With Family

Family can be one of the hardest spaces to live authentically. So many of us shrink ourselves to fit expectations that were never meant for us. But here's the truth: your authenticity matters more than their approval.

Yes, some conversations will be hard. Some connections might change. But living a life where you're pretending to be someone you're not? That's a slow death. It is also important to remember that authenticity is a two-way street. You can only expect authenticity from others if you are being authentic yourself. We can't choose our family. We all know that.

Ask yourself:

1. Am I being honest about what I need?
2. Am I showing up or hiding out?
3. Am I putting up a front?
4. Am I holding back what's going on in my life?
5. Am I living up to unrealistic expectations?
6. Am I doing things that don't align with my values?

It's not about winning arguments. It's about choosing yourself, with respect and clarity.

With Friends

We get to choose our friends. But are you choosing ones who see the real you?

I had a friend recently tell me she was reassessing her circle because she no longer felt like she could show up as herself. YES. That's the kind of evaluation we all need to do.

People are in your life for a season, a reason, or a lifetime. Once you know which one they are, act accordingly. Stop shrinking to keep the peace. Sometimes, you must leave people behind because they no longer serve you or where you are, and it's okay. Authenticity is more important than perfection, so take the time to be true to who you are.

Ask yourself:

- Do I feel free to speak honestly in this friendship?
- Do I feel drained or energized after we connect?
- Are we growing in the same direction?
- Do I show up as a version of myself that only represents what I want them to see? Or am I vulnerable when it's time to be?

Be real. Be open. And if someone can't handle your growth, that's their problem, not yours.

With Society

Being authentic in a world that profits from conformity is revolutionary. Yes, you'll face criticism. Yes, some people won't "get" you. And yes, it's still worth it.

Authenticity builds bridges. It sparks empathy. It challenges systems. When we each show up fully, we give society a shot at becoming something better.

It's important to know who's advocating for you. In the rooms you can't enter yet, who's speaking your name? Who's recommending you? Who sees you? If you don't know the answer to that, it's time to find out. Ask yourself:

1. Am I in environments where I'm valued?
2. Is my authentic self welcomed here?
3. Do I feel like I have to put on a mask to succeed?
4. How am I showing up?
5. Do I know who advocates for me when I am not in the room?

If you feel unwelcome or like you have to wear a mask around certain people in your life, you might need to make a shift. And you have permission to do just that.

With Yourself

Identity is defined by Oxford Languages as "the fact of being who or what a person or thing is." It is important to stop and ask yourself, who are you—really? Not your title. Not your job. Not your role in the family. Not the image you curate online. *You.*

Your identity is the foundation of your authenticity. But here's the kicker: most of us have never truly stopped to ask those deeper questions. So let's change that.

Ask yourself:

- How do people see me?
- How do I want to be seen?
- What part of me have I been hiding?
- What identity am I performing for others? And most importantly: *Why?*

Life is so short. Doesn't the world deserve to see you? The real you? Don't you deserve to be seen? Know who you are? How do you define identity? Think about the definition I listed and pause and answer these questions:

1. Who are you? Who do you want to be? Does it match?
2. Are you the parent you want to be?
3. What kind of spouse do you want to be?
4. What kind of friend do you want to be? We certainly can't leave you off.
5. What kind of employee do you want to be?

6. What kind of leader do you want to be?
    - Boss?
    - Manager?
    - Co-worker?
    - Teammate?
    - Committee member?
    - Student?

The list goes on. In answering these questions, you might realize that you are not showing up in some of these roles in the ways that you'd like. What is stopping you, and how important is this identity to living as authentically as possible?

I am often reminded about how short life is, and in those moments, I am forced to look in the mirror and say, "How are you showing up? What is your identity? How do people see you? Are you living as you want to be?" And in most cases, I am, but I will be honest: there are some areas of my life I know I am not. These are the moments when I must stop and identify what is truly holding me back. These moments are hard and can be life-changing if you decide to answer these questions and then *do* something about it, truly.

The person you are when no one's watching—that's your starting point. That's who the world deserves to see. So stop dimming your light. Stop apologizing. Be you. Fully. Freely. Unapologetically.

Now Commit and Be Unapologetically and Authentically You

My hope for you, dear reader, is that you go out into the world and show up as you. Unapologetically and authentically you. Without reservation. Without hurting others. We get one life—that's it. We don't know what tomorrow is going to bring. We were reminded of this during the COVID pandemic.

Our stories are still unfolding. My story is still unfolding. But my story so far has been one of me being me, and the consequences of that—whether good, bad, or indifferent. This is what life is all about—learning from our experiences. I don't apologize for being me, and I never will. What I will do is focus on learning from my relationships and experiences.

So, what's next?

ACTION CHANGES THINGS

REFLECT:

Can you commit to showing up as your authentic self?

1. Where in your life are you showing up as your full self?
2. Where are you shrinking, hiding, or pretending?
3. What relationships feel aligned with your authentic identity?

Quick Win: Write a commitment statement that starts with: *"I will show up unapologetically as myself by..."* (Go ahead—say it out loud. Claim it.)

"The world is waiting. I am waiting, and your true self is waiting - to show up!" —Paula R Jenkins

NOTES

Notes/References

The following sources helped inform selected definitions, research insights, data points, and reflection areas included throughout this book. They are organized by chapter to help readers locate the ideas, studies, and references connected to each section. Opening quotes are attributed in the chapters where known.

Introduction: What Is Authenticity and Why Does It Matter?

Ware, B. (2011). *The top five regrets of the dying: A life transformed by the dearly departing.* Hay House.

Wood, A. M., Linley, P. A., Maltby, J., Baliousis, M., & Joseph, S. (2008). The authentic personality: A theoretical and empirical conceptualization and the development of the authenticity scale. *Journal of Counseling Psychology, 55*(3), 385–399.

Chapter One: Unapologetically Me

Becker, H. S. (1963). *Outsiders: Studies in the sociology of deviance.* Free Press.

Chapter Two: Leading with Authenticity

Edmondson, A. C. (1999). Psychological safety and learning behavior in work teams. *Administrative Science Quarterly, 44*(2), 350–383.

Goleman, D. (1995). *Emotional intelligence: Why it can matter more than IQ.* Bantam Books.

Goleman, D. (1998). What makes a leader? *Harvard Business Review, 76*(6), 93–102.

Murtoff, J. (2025). Emotional intelligence. In *Encyclopaedia Britannica.* https://www.britannica.com/science/emotional-intelligence

Walumbwa, F. O., Avolio, B. J., Gardner, W. L., Wernsing, T. S., & Peterson, S. J. (2008). Authentic leadership: Development and validation of a theory-based measure. *Journal of Management, 34*(1), 89–126. https://doi.org/10.1177/0149206307308913

Chapter Three: Living Authentically

Harvard Business Review. (2019). The costs of code-switching. *Harvard Business Review.* https://hbr.org

Merriam-Webster. (n.d.). Communication. In *Merriam-Webster.com dictionary.* https://www.merriam-webster.com/dictionary/communication

Oxford Languages. (n.d.). Identity. In *Google English Dictionary.* Oxford University Press.

Reis, H. T., Sheldon, K. M., Gable, S. L., Roscoe, J., & Ryan, R. M. (2000). Daily well-being: The role of autonomy, competence, and relatedness. *Personality and Social Psychology Bulletin, 26*(4), 419–435. https://doi.org/10.1177/0146167200266002

Chapter Four: Being Financially Authentic

American Psychological Association. (2017). *Stress in America: The state of our nation.* https://www.apa.org

Federal Reserve Board. (2023). *Report on the economic well-being of U.S. households in 2022.* https://www.federalreserve.gov

LendingClub. (2023). *Paycheck-to-paycheck report.* https://www.lendingclub.com

Chapter Five: Communicating Authentically

Edelman. (2023). *2023 Edelman Trust Barometer global report.* https://www.edelman.com/trust

Goleman, D. (1995). *Emotional intelligence: Why it can matter more than IQ.* Bantam Books.

Goleman, D. (1998). What makes a leader? *Harvard Business Review, 76*(6), 93–102.

Mehrabian, A. (1971). *Silent messages.* Wadsworth Publishing.

Chapter Six: Social Media Authenticity

Bunker, C. J., Balcerowska, J. M., Precht, L.-M., Margraf, J., & Brailovskaia, J. (2024). Perceiving the self as authentic on social media precedes fewer mental health symptoms: A longitudinal approach. *Computers in Human Behavior, 152,* 108056.

Columbia Business School. (2020, October 6). Be yourself: Authenticity on social media leads to a happier life [Press release]. *CBS Newsroom.* https://business.columbia.edu/press-release/cbs-press-releases/be-yourself-authenticity-social-media-leads-happier-life

The Annie E. Casey Foundation. (2024, December 12). Effects of social media on mental health. https://www.aecf.org/blog/effects-of-social-media-on-mental-health

Chapter Seven: Praying with Authenticity

American Psychological Association. (n.d.). Religion and spirituality in coping with stress. https://www.apa.org

Emmons, R. A. (2007). *Thanks!: How the new science of gratitude can make you happier.* Houghton Mifflin.

Emmons, R. A., & McCullough, M. E. (2003). Counting blessings versus burdens: An experimental investigation of gratitude and subjective well-being in daily life. *Journal of Personality and Social Psychology, 84*(2), 377–389. https://doi.org/10.1037/0022-3514.84.2.377

Harvard Medical School. (2020). The relaxation response. *Harvard Health Publishing.* https://www.health.harvard.edu

Chapter Eight: Minding Your Authenticity

Azab, M. (2023, August 22). The history of imposter syndrome: Imposter syndrome isn't an official diagnosis—but it's still a real problem. *Psychology Today*. https://www.psychologytoday.com/us/blog/neuroscience-in-everyday-life/202308/the-history-of-imposter-syndrome

Rogers, C. R. (1961). *On becoming a person: A therapist's view of psychotherapy*. Houghton Mifflin.

Chapter Nine: Emotionally Intelligent Authenticity

Bradberry, T., & Greaves, J. (2009). *Emotional Intelligence 2.0*. TalentSmart.

Clance, P. R., & Imes, S. A. (1978). The imposter phenomenon in high-achieving women: Dynamics and therapeutic intervention. *Psychotherapy: Theory, Research & Practice, 15*(3), 241–247. https://doi.org/10.1037/h0086006

Korn Ferry Institute. (2021, April 23). Emotional intelligence: Why now? *Korn Ferry*. https://www.kornferry.com/institute/emotional-intelligence-why-now

Murtoff, J. (2025). Emotional intelligence. In *Encyclopaedia Britannica*. https://www.britannica.com/science/emotional-intelligence

Resources

Continue the journey. Scan here for companion resources, reflection tools, bonus content, and updates for *Show Up Like You Mean It*.

www.showuplikeyoumeanit.com

About the Author

Paula R Jenkins is known as The Lead By Example™ Speaker, a powerhouse in leadership development, emotional intelligence, and authentic communication. With a career that spans over two decades in corporate leadership, Paula traded in high-stress boardrooms and a 180/140 blood pressure reading for something far more impactful: helping leaders lead without losing themselves in the process.

As Founder and CEO of LFS Consulting LLC, Paula is on a mission to create courageous, heart-centered, and high-performing leaders. Her signature mantra, "True Leaders C.R.E.A.T.E.℠ More Leaders," guides her coaching, workshops, keynotes, and curriculum design. She has spoken to audiences across multiple industries, taught leadership-based strategies in college classrooms, and consulted for organizations.

A fierce advocate for personal truth, Paula teaches leaders that *everything begins and ends with communication*—but it doesn't end there. Through humor, real-talk storytelling, and a whole lot of passion, she helps leaders discover that their most powerful tool isn't their title—it's their ability to show up as themselves.

She holds an MBA in Leadership and Change Management from DePaul University, a B.S. in Computer Information Systems from Tuskegee University, and a laundry list of certifications she only mentions when absolutely necessary.

When Paula isn't coaching clients or lighting up a stage, you'll find her curating R&B playlists, mentoring the next generation of change-makers, or planning her next passport stamp with her sister-circles.